Michael Chandler is an Anglican priest who has served in the parochial ministry and is now Treasurer and senior Residentiary Canon of Canterbury Cathedral. His interest in church history in general, and the Oxford Movement in particular, has been sustained over many years. He is the author of biographies of two important Victorian churchmen, H. P. Liddon whose theology was the subject of his doctoral thesis, and J. M. Neale the hymn writer and controversialist.

An Introduction to the Oxford Movement

Michael Chandler

 CHURCH

Church Publishing Incorporated, New York

A catalog record for this book is available from
the Library of Congress

ISBN 0–89869–420–5

Church Publishing Incorporated
445 Fifth Avenue
New York, NY 10016
www.churchpublishing.org

5 4 3 2 1

Printed in Great Britain

To Janet, Tim and Debbie,
not forgetting Rhiannon and William

Contents

Introduction

The Oxford Movement in the nineteenth-century Church of England, like many reforming tendencies before and since, sought to get back to an original purity of vision. The deepest conviction of the men behind it was that the Church of England is catholic and reformed and not simply Protestant. It was an endeavour to reassert within the Church of England the catholicity of the earliest times and to secure the ancient doctrinal position, and its spiritual values, for their own generation. Fundamentally, it was a simple idea, but its execution was inevitably complex and it provoked opposition from those who were against its basic principle. Individuals on both sides sometimes seemed to be unaware that their opponents held, with equal fervour, different convictions.

Consequently, the story of the Movement is one of controversy, even though its originators, a small number of Oxford dons, were convinced of the peaceful nature of their motive. Indeed they were concerned with holiness of life, within the fellowship of Christ's Church, as essential for salvation. They were convinced that personal sanctity can only be achieved through orthodoxy of belief. Such orthodoxy could only be ensured if the integrity of the Church's doctrines were vigorously protected. The Movement was an endeavour to persuade the Church of England to renew its perception of its ancient heritage and authority, and to claim its rightful place as part of the Church catholic. As with holiness, sound learning was seen to be inseparable from the process. Similarly, worldliness was to be eschewed, and personal reputations were secondary to the great endeavour. These factors combined to make them state their case with considerable vigour and to fight hard for what they believed to be the essentials of the Christian faith.

The energy with which the Oxford men engaged in a movement which was to change Anglican self-understanding was fuelled by an awareness that they and the Church were under judgement. They perceived that the days were very evil and felt compelled to do what they could. It is easy for the historian to overstate the gravity of the situation in the Church of England during the early years of the nineteenth century. Within the Church there was a certain level of indifference to doctrine, but it may not have been as serious as John Henry Newman, and his friends Richard Hurrell Froude and John Keble, feared. It was certainly not as acute as historians of the Movement, until comparatively recently, tended to maintain. These distressing perceptions of church life were coupled with another fear, again not entirely justified that it was moribund. Worldliness was apparent in the Church, but the scandals were offset by the quiet examples of many conscientious clergy and devout lay people of considerable piety. The founders of what became known as the Oxford Movement were intensely serious in their Christian commitment and feared that the Church was under threat from an increasingly secularized society. This fear was compounded by the political situation. The Tories under the leadership of the Duke of Wellington were the traditional party of Church, state and monarchy, but in 1830 were ousted by the Whigs who sought to strengthen Parliament. The new administration was led by Lord Grey and was eager to establish itself as a reforming government. This turn of events made conservatively-minded churchmen particularly anxious. They expected that the reformers would soon fix their eyes upon the Church, which was living through one of the periodic phases of unpopularity that it has experienced. Newman and his colleagues were concerned with doctrinal and spiritual integrity but suspected that such considerations would not be respected by the secular zeal of the reformers. They concluded that drastic action was necessary if the Church of England were to recover its ancient authority, which was essential to a reassertion of its neglected catholicity. Only if it did so could it ensure the authentic proclamation of the gospel, and that the souls of men and women neither remained in jeopardy nor were further imperilled.

A generation before, the evangelicals had awakened the souls of many devout individuals. With notable exceptions, however, they had not been particularly successful in reaching those who occupied the pews of the Established Church. Nevertheless, the history of their work would always be a jewel in the Church's crown, but something more was needed as the Victorian age dawned. They had done relatively little to reinvigorate the Church as an institution. Newman, whose own spiritual origins lay in evangelicalism, was among the most able and among the first to recognize that a new force was required. He and his friends realized that the ancient catholic faith of the undivided Church was, paradoxically, that new force. What was needed was that which had been there all the time. It had served the souls of men and women for generations, but had been ignored within the Church of England and overlaid with additional dogmas in the Church of Rome, although Roman Catholicism was not their responsibility. They felt a call to restore the Church of England to a simple and apostolic vigour that was truly catholic. It was to this end that they deployed their considerable talents as theologians and, because it proved to be necessary, as controversialists. The history of the Movement was not straightforward, and was sometimes distressing. It reveals, however, a depth of conviction and perseverance in the face of misunderstanding, and sometimes misrepresentation, that was often heroic.

The story of that compound of heroism and opposition is what makes the Oxford Movement of such enduring fascination. As with all historical phenomena, that story assists later generations in their endeavours to understand how and why they came to be where they are, and this factor can enable those generations to see how modern problems might be approached.

Chapter 1

Origins of the Oxford Movement

When the Dean of St Paul's, a devout and pious man, described the origins of the Oxford Movement, his first sentence drew attention to the political situation in England. 'What is called the Oxford or Tractarian Movement began, without doubt, in a vigorous effort for the immediate defence of the Church against serious dangers, arising from the violent and threatening temper of the days of the Reform Bill'.[1] This was his considered opinion, for Richard William Church was looking back over more than 50 years. He wrote in the late 1880s about events in many of which he had been involved. His book, *The Oxford Movement: Twelve Years 1833–1845*, provided the first full historical account of the Movement. It gained a high and well justified reputation. It repaid the confidence which had inspired E. B. Pusey, the surviving founding father of the Movement, to ask him to write it. There had been, at the time, a sense almost of desperation among earnest churchmen who perceived the Church of England to be threatened by the plans of the government. They feared that erastianism, the control of ecclesiastical matters by the state, was about to become seriously detrimental to Christianity in England. Despite this fear, later generations have tended to emphasize the theological aspects of the situation rather than the political. Both perceptions are correct. There was real political danger, and the men of the Oxford Movement tried to fight it with theological weapons.

The common view of scholars of earlier generations was that the Church of England was virtually moribund spiritually in the early nineteenth century, but this has been attacked by more recent writers.

The upheavals of the previous 150 years had produced in many churchmen an attitude that was often described as 'high and dry'. It has become clear that this was not as desiccated as some of the Oxford Movement's supporters were later to suggest. Indeed, there is evidence that in the first 30 years of the nineteenth century there were signs of a revival of spirituality even among the more old-fashioned elements of the Church of England. Even so, there is much truth behind the view that the Church in the Hanoverian period had many worldly clergy and lay people. Some of the clergy were cynical in their acquisition and manipulation of lucrative appointments and in general the Church of England was significantly unpopular.

The evangelical revival of the late eighteenth century had seen energetic work done by devout and committed men and women, but belief among ordinary people was at a low ebb. Many of the educated classes were indifferent or even hostile to religion. Within the Church of England the evangelicals had concentrated their efforts in the parishes, and there were areas of real success. Inevitably, though, their emphasis on personal conversion, and salvation by individual faith, had limited their effectiveness across the Church as a whole. Historians of the Oxford Movement have often emphasized these flaws in order to present the revival in the best possible light. Indeed, some of the early protagonists of the Movement promoted the idea that the Church was in a parlous state before their intervention. An important lay enthusiast for Tractarianism who wrote in this vein was W. E. Gladstone, who claimed to report his personal experience.[2] Nevertheless, despite the obvious and sometimes well-publicized deficiencies, there continued to be a great deal of straightforward and conscientious public worship, preaching and pastoral care by the clergy. The situation was not clear-cut, but many sincere and earnest English churchmen believed that devotion was, at best, lukewarm. Others saw the problem not so much in terms of indifference, but more specifically as a threat to the future of the Church as an institution. They perceived a latent hostility waiting for its chance to undermine the Church and what it stood for. At the beginning of the 1830s this anxiety for the future of the Church of England coincided with an apparent threat from the government. Dean R. W. Church was correct to recognize the significance of political events. He also saw that there was a profound desire among some churchmen to raise the standards of worship and devotion generally. These factors together account for the essentially theological response of the originators of the Oxford Movement.

The instigators of the Movement were John Keble, John Henry Newman, Richard Hurrell Froude and Edward Bouverie Pusey. With their colleagues they were, first and foremost, Christian thinkers who recognized they were living in a Church under threat. They used their acumen as theologians to counter the threat by reasserting the neglected catholic roots of the Church of England. They recognized that, in a later phrase of Newman's about the Thirty-Nine Articles of Religion, 'God's good providence' had preserved the catholicity of the Church of England even through 'an uncatholic age'.[3] They also asserted the Church's own authority by seeking to make its spiritual and doctrinal origins apparent to the institution itself. It is necessary to explore the events that gave rise to what Dean Church called the 'violent and threatening temper' of an indifferent or hostile world. This process must include some analysis of the political situation of the years immediately before the Movement because, in large part, the ecclesiastical ferment arose from circumstances that affected the Church but were often beyond its control and outside its influence.

At the beginning of the nineteenth century, the Act of Union of England and Ireland was passed. As a result of this legislation, it became clear that Parliament could not ignore the suddenly increased numbers of Roman Catholics in the overall population, although they had previously ignored the small numbers in England and Wales. The new Act meant that approximately one third of the citizens of the newly united nation were not members of the Church of England.[4] This phenomenon meant that changes were inevitable, but they were slow in coming and did not follow any coherent pattern. Pressure for reform slowly mounted. The process of the removal of the political and civil disabilities of Roman Catholicism was slower than that for the removal of similar disabilities for Nonconformists. Dissenters were excluded from membership of the House of Commons by the seventeenth-century Test and Corporation Acts, but this disqualification was evaded by the passing of an annual Act of Indemnity. In 1828 this situation changed when the Acts themselves were repealed. The following April saw the passage of the Roman Catholic Emancipation Act. This was a more contentious piece of legislation than that of the previous year, which had gone largely unnoticed. Opposition to the removal of almost all civil disabilities from Roman Catholics was a sensitive issue and King George IV feared that, by signing the Act, he had broken his coronation oath. Other, less exalted, opponents of the Act regretted the extension of toleration to Roman Catholics. In part this was to do with long historical memories. The reign of Queen

Mary I had seen the persecution of Protestants, and that of King James II had ended in a constitutional crisis. The Emancipation Act of 1829 was a political necessity, if civil war in Ireland was to be avoided, whatever the personal feelings of private individuals and of the King and the Prime Minister.

The Prime Minister, the Duke of Wellington, was successful in his manoeuvre, but the process damaged the reputation of the Tory Party in England. As a consequence, the party lost a significant number of seats in the general election that took place at the end of June 1830 following the death of the King. George IV had not been the only man who disliked what Wellington had been compelled to do. Tory churchmen were not at all happy and began to fear for the future of the Church. The outcome of the general election increased their misgivings. Although Wellington formed a government after the election, by November 1830 it had fallen and the new Prime Minister was Earl Grey. He came to power at the head of a Whig administration that promised reform in the state and of the Church. Many churchmen who had disapproved of the legislation of the recent past were even more anxious as a new year dawned.

Lord Grey introduced his reforming plans immediately by bringing a Reform Bill before Parliament, but it did not survive. The King, now William IV, allowed Grey to go to the country and he achieved a working majority which enabled him to bring back the Bill. It was a genuinely reforming piece of legislation that sought to eradicate the so-called 'rotten boroughs'. These were parliamentary constituencies which were controlled by landowners or aristocrats whose influence enabled them to have their own nominees elected to seats in Parliament. The removal of rotten boroughs immediately abolished an important but often corrupt element of political patronage. The Act also improved the Parliamentary representation of the industrialized cities and increased the franchise to a limited extent. The First Reform Act (1832), as the measure became known, was an important landmark in British constitutional history. It is also important to Church historians because of the hostility which was generated against the already unpopular Church of England by the opposition of the bishops in the House of Lords. Initially the Lords rejected the Bill. Twenty-one bishops opposed it and six abstained. The majority of those bishops who opposed the Bill were not motivated simply by a desire to preserve the status quo. They saw themselves as active defenders of the constitution against those who wanted to sweep it away. Some of them were astute enough to wonder whether the

Church might be the next target of the Whigs and whether their own positions within the establishment might soon be threatened. The bishops constituted more than half the opposing majority and, when this was publicized, they incurred much opprobrium. Lord Grey had not expected that so many bishops would oppose him. The Lords in general and the bishops in particular attracted severe criticism not least from citizens who had been over-optimistic about the likely consequences of the legislation. Bishops were hissed and heckled, and even threatened with violence. Archbishop William Howley, who was surprised at the reaction to his opposition to the Bill, was mobbed in the streets of Canterbury and his chaplain complained that he had been struck in the face with a dead cat. Howley coolly observed that the man was fortunate that it was dead. The Bishop of Bath and Wells suffered the indignity of yokels throwing stones at his carriage. The Bishop of Carlisle was burnt in effigy. In Bristol a mob broke into the bishop's palace, damaged furniture and artefacts and burnt down the building.

In due course, the reintroduced Bill passed through Parliament and did receive sufficient support from the bishops. Indeed, no bishops opposed it at all on the third reading. The Church of England had, however, suffered damage to its reputation, and in the early 1830s critical pamphlets were produced and sold in large numbers. Some came from Dissenters who wanted to restore Christianity to a simplicity from which the Church seemed to be far removed. Others came from those who despised the Christian faith. There were many shades of opinion in between. The most effective critic was John Wade, who published *The Black Book* as a series of periodicals in the early 1820s. His master stroke was to rewrite some of them and to republish them some years later as *The Extraordinary Black Book*. Wade did not confine his strictures to the Church of England, but tackled many aspects of the establishment, including the aristocracy, the 'law and judicial administration', the 'Bank of England and the East India Company . . . pluralists, placemen, pensioners and sinecurists'. He was particularly aggressive towards the Church of England, criticizing the 'rapacity of the clergy', their non-residence, the 'revenues of the established Church', and the 'oppressiveness of the tithe system' and so on. The Church was accustomed to criticism. What was different on this occasion was the volume of it and the length of time that it held the public interest.

It was the year after the Reform Act when churchmen came under specific attack from the reforming zeal of Grey's government. In

February 1833 the Church Temporalities (Ireland) Bill came before the House of Commons. William Palmer of Worcester College, Oxford, was one who saw the danger. Ten years after the event he was to write in terms that Richard Church was later to echo, 'at the beginning of the summer of 1833, the Church of England and Ireland seemed destined to immediate desolation and ruin'.[5] The Irish Church Bill brought Palmer near to despair. The government was gripped by what he called 'a spirit of innovation' and Palmer felt that the Church was a victim, 'delivered over, bound hand and foot, into the power of a reckless Ascendancy; into the hands of a Parliament reckless of the high and sacred interests of religion . . . .'[6] There were two related aspects of reform that alarmed men such as Palmer. First, and of greatest importance, Palmer perceived the government's plans to be a threat to the doctrinal integrity of the Church of England. He believed that Parliament had no right to interfere with the Church's duty to order its own affairs. The second cause for alarm was financial. The Church of England enjoyed very considerable revenues but they were unevenly and unfairly distributed, as Wade had exposed. This anxiety soon became a real issue, and it had doctrinal overtones because of the way in which Grey's government set about this aspect of the reform.

Until it was disestablished in 1871, the Church in Ireland was part of the Church of England. Grey decided that 10 Irish dioceses were to be amalgamated, and that there would be a reduction of the revenues of two archbishoprics. In this way the Church's ridiculously top-heavy bureaucracy would be more appropriate to the tiny population to which it ministered. It represented, however, the suppression of half of the episcopate in Ireland. In all, funds were to be released totaling an estimated £150,000. The revenue would be cared for by a specially established Ecclesiastical Commission, but there were no concrete plans for its dispersal. The criteria under which these decisions about bishoprics and money were made seem to be reasonable enough in themselves. The anxiety was raised because of a fear for the Church itself within England. It appeared that the increasingly secularized House of Commons was involving itself in the regulation and possible disposal of Church assets. For many, but probably not the majority, it was outrageous that such alterations in the administration of the Church should be imposed without consultation. Some, like William Palmer, a careful and entirely orthodox scholar, held to the theological conviction that the secular authority had no right to interfere with the governance of the Church. They argued that the Church is a divinely founded society and that its reform was nothing to do with the secular government. For them the amalgamation of dioceses was seen to be of theological significance in that the secular arm was taking powers to decide on matters of spiritual jurisdiction and of pastoral care. The situation was complicated by the fact that the Church itself had no machinery for consultation or consideration. The nearest equivalent to such machinery was the Convocations of Canterbury and York which had not met since 1717. Consequently, those with a purist doctrine of the Church perceived this as a violation of its rights and a usurpation of its authority. There was also the ever-present and distinct fear that if the Whigs felt that they could succeed with reform of the Church in Ireland that they might turn their attention next to England itself. So economic interests coincided with theological principles.

On economic and pragmatic grounds, the proposals for the Irish Church were obviously sensible. Their doubtful nature only became apparent when they were measured against ecclesiastical independence and theological autonomy. The problem was that in England there was also a case to answer in respect of the need for reform. Critics of the Church could easily draw attention to the 'golden age of office hunters, bishops' favourites and relatives . . . .'[7] This criticism could still be levelled at the situation in the first decades of the nineteenth century. Richard Church made a careful comment which has tended to be overlooked by those anxious to present the Oxford Movement in stark contrast to what had gone before. He wrote that 'the Church, as it had been in the quiet days of the eighteenth century was scarcely adapted to the needs of more stirring times.'[8] This somewhat oversimplified picture comes from a man who was involved in what went on. He had been an undergraduate when Newman and Keble were at their most influential, but his view should not be allowed to obscure the genuine devotion that marked so many areas of life in the Church of England. This has been explored by a modern writer, Peter Nockles, in his book, *The Oxford Movement in Context*.[9] Such scholarship has since been eager to recognize the value of what had gone before the Oxford Movement. Indeed, it is possible to take this perception further and argue that the earnest-ness of men such as Richard Church, his friends and colleagues, with their later espousal of the Oxford Movement, were part of this process of revival.

The fears about political interference in the affairs of the Church of England which Dean Church recalled, were undoubtedly real. He was, in this respect, an old-fashioned Tory. He also recognized the more positive qualities of the Church in the Hanoverian period and rejoiced to describe them:

> There was nothing effeminate about it, as there was nothing fanatical; there was nothing extreme or foolish about it; it was a manly school, distrustful of high-wrought feeling and professions, cultivating self-command and shy of display, and setting up as its mark, in contrast to what seemed to it sentimental weakness, a reasonable and serious idea of duty.[10]

Even so, he recognized the need for greater holiness of life among serious believers. It was these elements, prominent in Richard Church's own character, that gave him the ability to analyse the threat posed by the Reform Bill. His was no uncritical acceptance of the view that the eighteenth-century Church of England had been compromised by its erastian relationship to the state. This is notwithstanding that by the time he wrote his great book, *The Oxford Movement: Twelve Years 1833–1845*, this had become a fashionable opinion among High Churchmen. Dean Church knew that much of the criticism was unfounded and he did not join in the general condemnation. His criticisms were measured, 'the typical clergyman . . . is represented, often quite unsuspiciously, as a kindly and respectable person . . .' who, sadly, was often 'not alive to the greatness of his calling'. But the picture Dean Church painted did include 'not only . . . gentle manners, and warm benevolence, and cultivated intelligence, but . . . simple piety and holy life'.[11] Unfortunately, whilst this picture of pastoral devotion is correct, the period had also been a 'golden age' for selfish exploiters of the wealth and social position of the Church of England. As such, it was easy for others to criticize. John Henry Newman himself seems to have been one such critic when seeking to demonstrate that the Oxford Movement was not only timely but also necessary to the survival of the Church of England. He saw the need for what he called a 'second Reformation'.[12]

In addition to the emerging Oxford Movement, it is important to notice that others were thinking hard about the problems facing the Church. By coincidence many of them were Fellows of Oriel College, the pre-eminent College in early-nineteenth-century Oxford. In contrast to the founding fathers of the Oxford Movement, several of them were theological liberals. They formed a loosely associated grouping who called themselves 'Noetics' and were, largely, what a later generation would call 'Broad Churchmen'. Richard Whately had been a prominent Noetic before his appointment as Archbishop of

Dublin. He was an eccentric who tried to teach his dog to climb trees, and a 'rough militant philosopher' who looked 'like a Yorkshire ostler'.[13] Like his associates, he was a supporter of the Whigs. Whately was one of Lord Grey's earliest episcopal appointments in 1831. Other Noetics included Edward Coplestone and Edward Hawkins, who were successively Provosts of the College. Another significant figure, whom we shall meet again, was R. D. Hampden. They saw themselves, as the nickname which they adopted implies, as intellectuals. They were eager to increase the comprehensiveness of the Church of England. There were, however, limits to their ambitions in this respect which were revealed when the Oxford Movement thinkers sought to extend that comprehensiveness in a direction which the Noetics did not like.

Among the theological liberals there was a feeling that there ought to be some relaxation of the degree of consent to the Thirty-Nine Articles. This was an important issue because 'subscription' to the Articles was required from everyone seeking admission to Oxford University. It was also a requirement for office holders within both universities and in the Church itself. Among recent publications had been a pamphlet by Richard Whately. He had written *Letters on the Church by an Episcopalian*, which had appeared anonymously, in 1826. Whately wrote in a clear style and with cogency, but his work was not influential in the long term. His understanding of the doctrine of the Church was largely conventional. He claimed that the Church was divinely founded and that its members stand in a given relation to each other and to Christ as its head. It has the right to expect, from the state, protection against violence and persecution. He ended with a liberal sentiment, a plea for disestablishment (but not disendowment). In this respect his argument played into the hands of the reforming Whigs. Later, John Henry Newman was to acknowledge an intellectual debt to Whately, but recognized that his mind was 'too different' from his own for them 'to remain long on one line'.[14]

Another of those who had given thought to the problems facing the Church was Thomas Arnold, the Headmaster of Rugby School and a former Fellow of Oriel. He came up with a simplistic and highly controversial suggestion in an article which subsequently became a notorious pamphlet, *The Principles of Church Reform*, which he published in January 1833 and which ran to several editions within six months. Arnold wanted all Christian believers brought under one umbrella organization. He asserted that the Church of England should make itself more comprehensive in order to embrace all except the

Roman Catholics, Quakers and Unitarians who, he was convinced, would not join. With this theory, he thought that the Church might be reformed in such a way as would guarantee its relevance and, as a result, preserve its place in the nation's life. To the theologically naive the scheme seemed to be a distant echo of Richard Hooker's view that the Church and the nation were as one. The passing of more than two centuries since Hooker's *Laws of Ecclesiastical Polity*, however, meant that his serious theological point about the nature of the Church in relation to the nation had become a practical impossibility. If Hooker's ideal had ever been realizable, it had been based on the assumption that Dissent would fade away and that Dissenters would be assimilated into the state Church.

Arnold's idea was based on the pragmatic view that the Church of England should become an all-embracing organization under which different religious opinions could be accommodated without much adaptation or change. Arnold's biographer, A. P. Stanley, summarized:

> if Dissenters were comprehended within the Establishment, the use of different forms of worship at different hours of the Sunday in the parish church, might tend to unite the worshippers more closely to the Church of their fathers and to one another.[15]

The passage of time, however, had enabled dissenting opinions to become theological systems in their own right, as it were, outside and in contrast to the Church of England. Even if it had at one time been a practical possibility, and it probably had not, by Arnold's time the idea was far too radical for serious consideration. Stanley went on to say that Arnold's suggestion was, by its opponents, 'torn from the context' and used to discredit the whole. In the anxious atmosphere of the time, Arnold's argument stood no chance of acceptance. On the contrary, it intensified the debate and was among the factors that prompted the Tractarians to respond with greater urgency. Arnold's article soon attracted attention. It was published exactly six months before the event that Newman later described as the start of the Oxford Movement. The fact that men such as Whately and Arnold were concerned reveals that the Church of England was thought to be in a serious condition by others than those who initiated the Oxford Movement. Indeed, Arnold himself declared that 'the Church as it now stands no human power can save'.[16] This view was not widely held, even by his fellow Noetics, but there had grown up a degree of scepticism about the Christian faith and the Church of England's presentation of it.

This was the scene at Oxford in the early 1830s. The Oriel Noetics were liberal or Whig in their theological and political views. They wanted some relaxation of the restrictions which they believed stifled theological debate. Consequently, they were not sympathetic to others who believed that there should be a renewed emphasis on ancient traditional Christian theology. The instigators of the Oxford Movement wanted exactly that. They fought for a return to the doctrines of the early Church of the patristic period, and a recognition of the importance of the Caroline divines who had articulated classical Anglicanism two centuries before.

John Henry Newman was a Fellow of Oriel and was destined to be the most significant figure in the early stages of the Oxford Movement. Newman was born on 21 February 1801. He came from an evangelical background and his father was a banker. Newman senior had been unsure whether to send his son to Oxford or to Cambridge and decided on the former at the last moment. He made a choice that was to have very significant consequences for his son and for the Church of England. Young Newman studied as an undergraduate at Trinity College. He was a highly strung, intense individual who was acutely aware that he was called by God to be a priest and to remain unmarried in God's service. He was elected to his Fellowship in 1822. He retained his Fellowship when, six years later, he succeeded Edward Hawkins as vicar of the University church of St Mary when Hawkins was elected Provost of the College. At St Mary's his considerable gifts as a preacher established his reputation as a creative thinker. His sermons were published as *Parochial and Plain Sermons* in eight volumes between 1834 and 1842, and had a profound effect far beyond the vicinity of Oxford.

Newman was invited, in 1831, to write a book on the Councils of the early Church. The invitation came from Hugh James Rose, the Cambridge-educated rector of Hadleigh in Suffolk who, with W. R. Lyall, later the Dean of Canterbury, was co-editor of a planned library of theological works. Newman began his research in the long vacation of 1831 and by the end of August informed Rose that it was necessary to write first about the Arian heresy of the fourth century. In the event, Rose, with Archdeacon Lyall his co-editor, concluded that Newman's book was not suitable for inclusion in their series. It was a history of the heresy and not of the Councils set up to deal with it. Interestingly, Lyall thought that parts of it were too sympathetic to Roman Catholicism, but the main concern was that it was too specialized. It was a competent piece of work and it was accepted for publication by

Rivingtons. It was ready by July 1832, but did not come out until the end of the following year.[17]

Newman had lost his sympathy for the liberals and was no longer attached to Whately as a friend and a mentor, having changed his views at the time of 'the great Reform Agitation'.[18] The 'Whigs had come into power; Lord Grey had told the bishops to set their house in order' and so 'the vital question was how are we to keep the Church from being liberalised?'[19] He felt that if liberalism were to gain a footing, then the Church as he knew it would be lost, and that what he called 'Reformation principles' would be powerless to protect it.[20] He was at a loss as to how he should react whilst, at the same time, being desperate to do something. Late in 1832, Newman 'was easily persuaded to join Hurrell Froude and his father, who were going to the south of Europe for the health of the former'.[21]

Froude was born in 1803 and was always known by his middle name. Although he was a little younger than Newman, the two influenced each other greatly and Newman was devastated by his early death in 1836 from consumption. Theologically and politically Hurrell Froude was a conservative. He was handsome, had a brilliant intellect, a lively quick-witted manner, and an intense piety. Consequently he wielded an influence which was greater than would normally have been the case with such a young man. He had been educated at Oriel College and had been elected a Fellow in 1826 and was appointed a tutor the following year. He was one of the founders of the Oxford Movement and it was Froude who brought together John Keble, who had taught him, and Newman.

Froude, through his friendships with Keble and Newman, was to be one of the formative minds in the Movement, despite his early removal from the scene. He was the eldest son of Robert H. Froude, an old-fashioned churchman who was rector of Dartington and Archdeacon of Totnes. A landowner in his own right and a magistrate, the elder Froude exemplified the weaknesses of the old system, but he also exemplified its strengths with his unfussy piety, and well-developed sense of justice and devotion to the Church of England along with his practical belief in its doctrines.

Richard Hurrell Froude carried his father's beliefs to a new level of expression and modified them according to his own insights. These he gained from his reading of patristic texts and from his reflections upon the true nature and vocation of the Church of England. He was to be the author of several of the *Tracts for the Times*. His private thoughts were confided to his diary and were to make considerable difficulties when they were published after his death. But all this was in the future. By 1832 he was already ill, having caught a chill sleeping in the open on the deck of an Isle of Wight ferry. Froude's father was very anxious about his son's health and he decided that the young man might benefit from a trip to the Mediterranean. Newman was invited to join them, but being the man he was, hesitated momentarily on the grounds that he did not want to intrude on a family party. He was, however, attracted by the thought of foreign travel and this, with his regard for Froude, overcame the hesitation. An additional attraction in going away was the fact that the proposed trip released him from a complicated situation at Oriel. He was eligible for election to the office of Dean, the Fellow who was responsible for college discipline. The Dean of Oriel was also Vice-Provost. Newman suspected that if he were elected he would come into conflict with Provost Hawkins over the vexed matter, as he perceived it, of compulsory under-graduate attendance at Holy Communion. Hawkins saw nothing wrong in the practice, but Newman was strongly opposed to compul-sion. His absence on the Mediterranean trip at the time of the election meant that he could avoid the possibility of defeat in the election as well as any disagreeable consequences of victory.

They sailed from Falmouth on 8 December 1832 and Newman sent home many descriptive letters. With Froude, he called on Nicholas Wiseman, the future cardinal, in Rome 'at the Collegio Inglese' where there were some theological indiscretions in their discussion. He had some minor adventures and, with Froude, wrote a number of poems. They were published, with poetry by John Keble and others, in the *British Magazine* under the collective title, *Lyra Apostolica*. He parted from the Froudes at Rome in order to make a second visit to Sicily. There he suffered an illness which lasted for three weeks. He was for-tunate in being well looked after by a servant named Gennaro. All the while, and particularly as he recovered his health, Newman nurtured his sense that he should do something for the Church on his return. Indeed, he sat on his bed and surprised the faithful Gennaro by break-ing down in tears. When questioned by his valet he could only answer, 'I have a work to do in England',[22] a remark similar to one made earlier in Rome to Wiseman. He had plenty of time to think about what it might be because he was forced to wait another three weeks for a ship that took him to Marseilles. Further delays occurred when the vessel was becalmed, and it was at this time he wrote various poems, including the one best known by its opening line, 'Lead kindly light'. It was a poem that reveals the influence of Romanticism on

Newman and it touched the sensibilities of many of his contemporaries. It does not, however, reflect his anxiety or his eagerness to tackle the situation. He arrived at his mother's house on 9 July, a few hours after his brother Francis had returned from Persia.

Many years later Newman wrote a spiritual autobiography which he called *Apologia pro vita sua*. There he recorded that it was on the Sunday following his return, 14 July, that things suddenly came together. His views crystallized, and for him the Oxford Movement began. He wrote, 'I have ever considered and kept the day, as the start of the religious movement of 1833'.[23] The human agent for Newman's epiphany was John Keble (1792–1866). Keble was described, by a largely hostile commentator, as 'a representative of the devout mind of England'.[24] He had also been a Fellow of Oriel College, but he held very different theological opinions from the Noetics. Like Froude he was an old-fashioned Tory and the son of a High Church parson of the old school. Keble's background was entirely conventional. He always revered the judgement of his father, who was also called John, and this is a factor that must be remembered when assessing his mind. It was from his father that Keble had first learnt to appreciate and believe in the values and theology of classical Anglicanism. This had been articulated in the seventeenth century by men known collectively as the Caroline divines. The elder John Keble was a country clergyman and his son was to have a similar ministry for most of his life, although he was often not far from controversy. He was the oldest of the originators of the Oxford Movement and certainly did not set out to found a movement or to lead a protest. He simply did his duty as he perceived it, but in so doing shared in a remarkable and profound chain of events. Ultimately this was to change permanently the way in which the Church of England understood itself. It had consequences also for the way in which it presented the Christian faith to the world. He shared with his mentors a full grasp of the doctrine of the visible Church, the apostolic succession, the real presence of Christ in the Eucharist and the other doctrinal tenets which they expressed in Anglican form.

John Keble had gone up to Oxford, aged only 14, after being educated at home by his father, and had a brilliant career at Corpus Christi College. This culminated in his election, when he was 19, to his Fellowship at Oriel in 1811, by coincidence on the same day as Whately. Keble mixed as an equal with the leading intellectuals and could have progressed to high office in the Church or in national life. His contemporaries were impressed by his modesty and humbled by his devout nature. An insight into this aspect of Keble's character was unwittingly given by Newman in 1827 when he had voted against Keble and supported Hawkins in the election for the new Provost of Oriel. Newman, who later came to regret the way in which he had voted, observed, 'you know we are not electing an angel but a Provost'.[25] Keble was ordained deacon in 1815 and priest in 1816 and made a tutor at Oriel in 1817. In 1823, however, he resigned his University posts and returned to his aged father's rural parish to help out as a curate. He did not abandon intellectual work, nor did he abandon Oxford, and in 1831 was elected Professor of Poetry and held that office for 10 years. He delivered his lectures in Latin, and they were eventually published in 1844, although an English translation was not forthcoming until many years after the author's death. The lectures consisted of a sympathetic criticism of the principal Latin and Greek poets. A major theological undertaking by Keble was completed in 1836 after six years' work. It was a three-volume edition, with a substantial introduction, of the works of Richard Hooker, the most important of the Caroline divines.

Keble had, in the opinion of Richard Church, 'nothing very unusual in his way of life, or singular and showy in his work as a clergyman; he went in and about among the poor, he was not averse to society'. In 1835, when he got married, Newman was rude about it in a letter to another friend and later called marriage 'a very second rate business'.[26] Keble, however, was very happy and got on with his ministry. Dean Church wrote, 'he preached plain, unpretending, earnest sermons; he kept up his literary interests. But he was a deeply convinced Church-man, finding his standard and pattern of doctrine and devotion in the sober earnestness and dignity of the Prayer Book . . .'. A little later Church continued, 'there was nothing in him to foreshadow the leader of a bold and wide-reaching movement. He was absolutely without ambition'.[27] He was the archetypal Anglican clergyman, being prop-erly pious, self-effacing and with a pastoral heart linked with a love of sound learning. His habit of avoiding the 'showy' in his sermons was due to a conviction that a preacher should not allow his personality to draw the attention of his hearers away from the Christian message. Consequently he was often dull in his presentation. It was, however, the very same conservative qualities in Keble's personality that were to propel him into speaking his deepest thoughts. He did not see himself as a controversialist, but events were to demonstrate that he did not shirk conflict when he believed it to be necessary. Politically, like all High Churchmen at the time, he was a Tory, so the proposals put forward by Earl Grey were opposed to Keble's political principles. Unusually, his old-fashioned traditionalist view of the Church as a spiritual corporation meant that he was uneasy with its established place in English society. Keble's conservatism was, therefore, simultaneously radical. He would not keep silent when he saw the state about to lay secular hands upon the sacred edifice of the Church. In this sense, he was close to the non-jurors who, after the exile of King James II, preferred to be misunderstood than to accept compromise when William III and Mary II came to the throne in 1688.

To this picture of theological seriousness and quiet but stubborn integrity needs to be added the fact that Keble was a poet. To the modern mind his poetry often seems rather bland and pietistic, but in its own day it was very popular. In 1827 he published, anonymously and only at the insistence of his father and some friends, and very much against his own modest judgement, a volume of verses related to the collects and readings for Holy Communion within the Book of Common Prayer. It had as its title *The Christian Year*. It was to be his principal poetic publication and contains material which is still familiar; 'New every morning is the love', 'Sun of my soul' and 'Bless'd are the pure in heart' are the most well-known examples. He also produced a volume of poetry with the title *Lyra Innocentium* and another called *Miscellaneous Poems*. Poetry by John Keble was included in the collection known as the *Lyra Apostolica*, but it was *The Christian Year*, theoretically an anonymous publication, which established his reputation and led to his professorship. It was enormously successful and had made him well known before the Oxford Movement brought him before the public eye. Eventually the royalties made a large contribution to the restoration work of Hursley parish church where Keble served as vicar from 1836 until his death 30 years later. The book, through which 'the expressions of a romantic age . . . entered Christian devotion'[28] had run to 95 editions by the end of Keble's life, and that total leapt to 109 in the year after he died.

It was in 1833, however, that John Keble unexpectedly achieved lasting fame. He did so through the improbable medium of his Assize Sermon. John Keble was an unlikely warrior and for him, of all people, a sermon was an unlikely weapon. It was his duty to preach the Assize Sermon in the University pulpit of St Mary's Church in Oxford on Sunday 14 July. He did not shirk that duty. The sermon was published with the title 'National Apostasy'. Its effect was convulsive because it was the catalyst for Newman's thinking, as he acknowledged so readily. In his opinion it triggered the Oxford Movement.

Chapter 2

Early Progress

John Keble decided that his Assize Sermon should speak out against the 'helpless state of the Church of England', as he described it later in a letter.[1] He was concerned that contemporary secularized society had little time for the Church, and even less understanding of its spiritual purpose and theological status. For Keble the Whig government's proposal for the Church in Ireland located the problem at the intersection of religion and politics, just as Dean Church was to explain in 1890. Everyone knew that the Church in Ireland was in a parlous state compared to England. In the latter the problem was indifference and disbelief, in Ireland it was difference of belief. Only a small proportion of the Irish population were members of the Church of England, but the Church held rich endowments of bishoprics and rectories and ministered only to a minority. Grey's government sought to remove some of the anomalies. The Irish Church Temporalities Bill introduced wide-ranging reforms, some of which were financial. In theological terms, the most important changes were the amalgamation of 10 dioceses, including two archbishoprics, with other dioceses nearby. Churchmen such as Keble and his friends were convinced that the reform of dioceses could only be addressed by the Church itself and believed the government's proposals to be both impious and sacrilegious. Action by the legislature was inappropriate and, as such, must be resisted by the Church.

This was the situation when he was invited by the Vice-Chancellor to preach the Summer Assize Sermon. Keble's first biographer observed that 'gentle as he was by nature, and loving-hearted to individuals . . . it was not in his nature, nor according to his conscience, to be inactive when he felt deeply'.[2] So it was that Keble was glad to have an opportunity to speak. His concern was wider than simply the Irish situation created by Lord Grey. He was keen to be recognized as addressing a bigger question than solely the lost cause of the Irish bishoprics. It may be that that is why the proposed legislation was not mentioned in the sermon, but Keble's subtlety of mind may be the true reason. Keble was aware that he was addressing a congregation made up largely of laymen, who occupied positions of influence and respon- sibility. He pointed out that theirs was the primary role and duty to make sure that changes within society were in accord with the precepts of the Christian Church. Keble's text was 1 Samuel 12.23, and he argued that the Old Testament provided appropriate models for civil actions in public life, particularly at times when 'public duties, public errors and public dangers are in question'.[3]

Because of its lack of a specific reference to the Irish Church Temporalities Bill, the sermon can readily be interpreted as address- ing the whole political situation in relation to the Church's role in nineteenth-century society. The Preface to the first printed edition of the sermon, however, did contain a strong but nevertheless oblique reference to the legislation:

> Since the following pages were prepared for the press, the calamity, in anticipation of which they were written, has actually overtaken this portion of the Church of God. The legislature of England and Ireland, (the members of which are not even bound to profess belief in the Atone- ment,) this body has virtually usurped the commission of those whom our Saviour entrusted with at least one voice in making ecclesiastical laws, on matters wholly or partly spiritual.[4]

He then proceeded to the admission that examples might not be pleasing to those who would prefer to conduct the affairs of a nation 'even a Christian nation', without God and 'without His Church'.[5] As the argument progressed, Keble asked what he clearly regarded as two fundamental questions and in the remainder of the sermon set out to answer them.

First, he asked, 'What are the symptoms by which one may judge most fairly, whether or no a nation, as such, is becoming alienated from God and Christ?' He acknowledged that such could happen, and went on to argue that the most likely grounds for such a change to come about would be 'by some pretence of danger from without'.[6] Relating this to the world of the Old Testament, Keble cited a number of examples of how the Israelites had failed to meet their commitments as the people of God. He then continued, 'so, in modern times, when liberties are to be taken, and the intrusive passions of men to be indulged, precedent and permission, or what sounds like them, may easily be found and quoted for everything'.[7] He then came fairly close to identifying the actual matter that was exercising him. It was a larger issue than just the Irish Church Bill, it was the whole religious tenor of the age:

> the growing indifference . . . to other men's religious sentiments. Under the guise of charity and toleration we are come almost to this pass; that no difference, in matters of faith, is to disqualify for our approbation and confidence, whether in public or domestic life. Can we conceal it from ourselves, that every year the practice is becoming more common, of trusting men unreservedly in the most delicate and important matters, without one serious inquiry, whether they do not hold principles which make it impossible for them to loyal to their Creator, Redeemer and Sanctifier?[8]

Being the man he was, John Keble did not want to be more specific. He was concerned with the integrity of public life and believed it to be of an unacceptably lower standard than in previous generations. The contents of the Irish Church Bill, which was put forward by men who believed themselves to be Christian, demonstrated this conclusively to Keble. Although he did not say so in the sermon, he saw the proposed legislation as a deliberate attempt to undermine the Church. It was an attack on its freedom and on its chief pastors, the bishops. This was the core of his argument. He believed that bishops exercised a divinely authorized ministry and that the proposed legislation robbed them of their authority. He said, 'disrespect to the Successors of the Apostles, as such, is an unquestionable symptom of enmity to Him, Who gave them their commission at first, and has pledged Himself to be with them for ever'.[9] Keble then turned to the second question which he had earlier identified and asked, 'And what are the particular duties of sincere Christians, whose lot is cast by Divine Providence in such a time of dire calamity?'[10] A little later he continued, 'How may a man best reconcile his allegiance to God and his Church with his duty to his country, that country, which now, by the supposition, is fast becoming hostile to the Church?' And here he revealed the whole basis of his reasoning by drawing the conclusion that hostility to the Church meant that such a country 'cannot therefore long be the friend of God'.[11]

The fundamental message of Keble's sermon was that the Church of England represents the universal Catholic Church and has a genuinely apostolic ministry. It was not the creature of Parliament and therefore could not be legitimately interfered with by the government. It was the same message that Newman was to convey to a different public in *Tract I* which came out less than two months later. At the time, the sermon attracted little interest. It gained some momentum when Keble published it and circulated it among his friends, although Pusey did not read the copy which he received 'From the author'; its pages remained uncut after his death. It was Newman who believed that the Assize Sermon by John Keble actually started the Oxford Movement. In reality, however flattering Newman's opinion of the sermon, it was but one of the sparks which ignited the Movement. Perhaps its real significance for Newman was that it gave him the comfort of knowing that he was not alone in his anxiety. That may have been sufficient to motivate him but, at the time, no one suspected that John Keble had started a revolution on that summer afternoon.

July 1833 was to see another event of significance. A fortnight after Keble's sermon, a meeting was held at Hadleigh in Suffolk. It is mentioned in all histories of the Oxford Movement, largely because 'eight years later it came to be charged with concocting a secret plot to alter the doctrines and discipline of the Church of England'.[12] Hugh James Rose (1795–1838), the rector of Hadleigh, was the man behind the meeting which lasted several days. He was an old-fashioned High Churchman who had been educated at Trinity College, Cambridge, where he had earned distinction. He served as a parochial clergyman, but was also an active journalist. In 1832 he had founded the *British Magazine and Monthly Register of Religious and Ecclesiastical Information*, mainly to provide a platform for the theological views which he found congenial. Thomas Mozley was impressed by Rose, and described him as 'the one commanding figure and a very lovable man, that the frightened and discomfited Church people were now rallying round'.[13] Dean Church obviously admired him: 'he had the prudence, but not the backwardness, of a man of large knowledge, and considerable experience of the world . . . he showed his courage and his unselfish earnestness in his frank sympathy'. During the remainder of his comparatively short life, Rose took little part in the Oxford Movement although he was sympathetic to its earlier phase. Dean Church thought that, had he lived, Rose would eventually have been 'one of the chiefs'.[14]

The first thing to notice about the Hadleigh Conference is that it consisted of only four individuals, although they were 'more or less like-minded'.[15] They were Rose, A. P. Perceval, 'upright, cantankerous

. . . somewhat lacking in tact', William Palmer of Worcester College 'learned and dignified'[16] and a man of 'exact and scholastic mind, well equipped at all points in controversial theology, strong in clear theories and precise definitions'.[17] The fourth man at the Conference, R. H. Froude, was a man of a very different cast of mind. Rose had a curate, R. C. Trench, later Archbishop of Dublin, who attended some or perhaps all of the gatherings, but his later recollections were not entirely accurate. Neither Keble nor Newman went to the Hadleigh meeting. Indeed, Keble had been expected, but decided against attending because he mistakenly thought that it was about increasing the circulation of the *British Magazine*. Both of them, however, were in active correspondence with those who were there. Of the group, Palmer was the most profound theologian. Palmer and Perceval both left descriptions of the meeting, Palmer in his *Narrative of Events*, and Perceval in *A Collection of Papers*.

The group met in a fine panelled room in the Gateway Tower of Rose's home. They agreed that the situation facing the Church was urgent. The doctrine of the apostolic succession and the integrity of the Book of Common Prayer were the chief things for which they agreed to strive. Palmer wrote,

> the conference at Hadleigh, which continued for nearly a week, concluded without any specific arrangements being entered into: though we all concurred as to the necessity of some mode of combined action, and the expediency of circulating tracts or publications on ecclesiastical subjects.[18]

One activity, which Dean Church thought was Palmer's idea, was to form an association or league for the defence of the Church of England. Unfortunately, it is not possible to identify who thought of it, either from Palmer's own account or from that of Perceval, so it seems likely that Church got this information personally from Palmer himself. Dean Church compared those early plans for the Association for the Defence of the Church with the English Church Union and Church Defence Association. Both organizations were founded later in the nineteenth century but were active nationally by the time he wrote. The plan withered, probably because there was a vacuum in the leadership of the nascent movement at that moment. Also, Hurrell Froude was opposed to the whole idea of such associations. Richard Church recorded, 'plans of Association' were drawn up but came to nothing. 'The endeavour brought out differences of opinion – differences as to the rightness or the policy of specific mention of doctrines; differences as to the union of Church and State'.[19] Palmer was more frank than Dean Church and blamed the failure of the idea on Oxford politics, which stopped the circulation of papers 'advising the formation of societies', and it was he who said that the objections were raised by Froude and Newman.[20] Their opposition stemmed, on Froude's part in particular, from a rejection of the concept of 'any society or association other than the Church itself'.[21] They both feared that such groups would take the initiative away from the more personal and dynamic sort of action that they wanted and were unlikely to produce results. Palmer nevertheless spoke about forming local associations to groups of clergy in Coventry, Winchester and London.

A second and more successful plan was to produce a declaration. In effect this was a secondary development of the idea of associations. Eventually a document was produced in the form of an 'Address' to Archbishop Howley. It was signed by 7,000 clergy and was presented to Howley in February 1834 by what H. P. Liddon called an 'influential deputation'. A similar address from lay members of the Church to the Archbishop was signed by 230,000 'heads of families' and this was presented in the following May. Joshua Watson was involved in the preparation of both addresses. He advised the compilers of the clerical address, and composed that from the laity. Watson was a devout, wealthy and philanthropic layman of the old-fashioned High Church school. He devoted himself to the Church of England after retiring early from a business career. His brother was rector of Hackney, in those days a village. With their like-minded friends, they became known as the 'Hackney Phalanx' or Clapton Sect. Joshua Watson lived at Clapton from 1811 and the nickname was a conscious adaptation of that of the earlier evangelical group which was known as the Clapham Sect. Although the idea for the clerical Address was aired at Hadleigh, it is clear that the work was done later.

The other idea of 'tracts or publications on ecclesiastical subjects' came quickly to fruition and 25 Tracts were published before the Declarations were presented. They were to give the Movement an identity and a title. The motive was to set out the case that the Church is a divinely-founded society and to defend all the doctrinal implications that flowed from it. As such it needed to be defended against the Whiggish erastian view that it was merely part of the state establishment.

Newman took over the idea and quickly made it his own. It may simply be that the idea had in fact occurred simultaneously to him and to the Hadleigh group. It was, after all, hardly an original one. The publication of theological pamphlets certainly appealed to Newman's scholarly mind. At first, he thought that they should be short. He told Perceval 'A tract would be long enough if it filled four octavo pages'.[22] Such publications on religious matters were commonplace, but they had a bad reputation among serious and learned people so the appeal was, in part, to Newman's sense of irony. Such pamphlets often suffered from 'disparaging associations' because they were usually unscholarly and often trivial in their content. Newman set to work on the first *Tract for the Times*, 'Thoughts on the Ministerial Commission respectfully addressed to the Clergy'. One of his reasons for not wanting an association was that he did not want the Tracts to be controlled by anyone other than their authors, nor did he want them to be composed by committees. He said that he wanted to preserve the freedom of the individual writer and it is clear that he did not want any external restraints on his own work. He may have felt that the liberty of each author was a price worth paying in order to preserve his own freedom of expression. At that moment particular gifts

> were required to stir the minds of Churchmen in general . . . The needed qualities were contributed by Newman . . . And the majority of the Tracts, the earliest and the most important, were the work of Newman. It was his power of speech and writing, combined with his enthusiasm, practical energy, and attractive personality, which could alone supply the necessary impetus at the start.[23]

What the Church and the country really wanted was plain speaking which could not be achieved through manifestos or committees. It was necessary for each individual to write and to speak for himself, whilst working in co-operation with like-minded colleagues. The first three *Tracts for the Times* were all from Newman's pen. They were dated 9 September 1833 and were directed at the clergy. Later this led to the view that 'the Tractarians were essentially a clerical party'.[24] It would be incorrect to claim that the Oxford Movement was exclusively clerical. However, it was because it addressed itself initially to the clergy as leaders of the Church in their localities that the teaching of the Tractarians was eventually to exert such a lasting and profound influence on the Church of England as a whole.

It soon became apparent that it was one thing to publish pamphlets in the hope of starting a debate, or even to stop a government revolution, but it was quite another to disseminate the published material. At this time Newman was feeling excited and dynamic. Friends allegedly did not recognize in him the man who had gone to the Mediterranean with the Froudes. He had fully recovered his health and knew that he was full of a new-found vitality. This was strengthened by

> the consciousness that I was employed in the work which I had been dreaming about, and which I felt to be so momentous and inspiring. I had a supreme confidence in our cause: we were upholding that primitive Christianity which was delivered for all time by the early teachers of the Church, and which was registered and attested in the Anglican formularies and by the Anglican divines.[25]

Newman himself, and others whom he encouraged, persuaded booksellers to stock the *Tracts for the Times* and also called on clergy in the hope of getting them to buy copies for themselves and others. In his *Apologia*, Newman described this process, 'I called upon clergy in various parts of the country, whether I was acquainted with them or not, and I attended at the houses of friends where several of them were from time to time assembled'.[26] A little later he described how Oxford graduates who had become country curates also persuaded local booksellers to stock the Tracts. He described how they 'got them into newspapers, introduced them to clerical meetings, and converted more or less their rectors and brother curates'.[27] Within a relatively short time, Rivingtons took over publishing the Tracts and the problem of distribution disappeared for the authors. Initially they sold well, but by the autumn of 1836 Rivington told Newman that they were not selling and that he wished to give up publishing them.[28]

Thomas Mozley wryly described his own experience in the earlier period. 'Putting on a greatcoat and mounting a shaggy pony at the dawn of a winter's day, I rode with a bundle of tracts'. At one vicarage 'the front door was promptly opened by a wonderfully handsome man, much over ninety, asking shortly what I wanted, and looking askance at the hoof marks of my pony on his smooth gravel'. Mozley on that occasion was fortunate to receive both breakfast and a list of potential buyers of his wares, along with an introduction to the son of his host.[29] Newman said he did 'not think that much came of such attempts' and added 'nor were they quite in my way'.[30] He was similarly dismissive of the effectiveness of the letters that he wrote to clergy commending the Tracts. Gradually, interest was kindled in the *Tracts for the Times*, although not all the readers agreed with the possibility that the Church of England might be in danger from the reforming zeal of the Whigs. Curiosity about the Tracts was increased by the obvious contrast between their content and that which was customary in such publications. Dean Church made the point:

> The ring of these early Tracts was something very different from anything of the kind yet known in England. They were clear, brief, stern appeals to conscience and reason, sparing of words, utterly without rhetoric, intense in purpose. They were like the short, sharp, rapid utterances of men in pain and danger and pressing emergency.[31]

The early *Tracts for the Times* were successful in their aim to startle their readers with their restatement of largely forgotten claims about the Church of England's theological foundations.

Newman and his fellow authors saw themselves as encouraging the clergy of the Church of England to reassert their historical and theological heritage in the face of the threat of erastianism and liberalism. The doctrines and traditions which the Tracts espoused were, the writers claimed, no more than the historical heritage of the Church of England, but it was a neglected heritage. Consequently, it seemed strange to many who encountered it for the first time when they read the Tracts. To such people the novelty seemed foreign and antiquarian and, therefore, 'Roman'. Inevitably, the Tracts aroused opposition. The loose accusations of Romanism indicated something of the seriousness of the situation. Among their opponents were some who saw the Tracts as an endeavour to undo the Reformation; their response was the old accusation of 'popery'. One later commentator attributed the reaction to intellectual custom and the slackening of the habit of the clergy with regard to professional reading. Part of the agitation caused by the Tracts was due to the anonymity of the authors. This was a deliberate decision by Newman in the first Tract, which was addressed *ad clerum*. He wrote, 'I am but one of yourselves – a Presbyter; and therefore I conceal my name, lest I should take too much on myself by speaking in my own person. Yet speak I must; for the times are very evil'. What Newman established also became the normal practice of other authors. Although they were not the products of an Association, nevertheless it soon became clear that the Tracts were associated with each other. Readers were intrigued by the mystery surrounding anonymous scholarly and incisive essays which were published in the popular, but normally unscholarly medium of inexpensive short pamphlets.

The veil of anonymity soon became thin. In the meantime it added to the excited nature of the response the Tracts generated, and they soon became known as the Oxford Tracts, a factor that made for difficulties later. It soon became an open secret that the first Tracts were from Newman's pen, but it was soon apparent to assiduous readers that other writers were contributing to the burgeoning series. Within three months no less than 17 Tracts were published, of which eight were from Newman's pen. John Keble contributed the fourth in the series. It had as its title 'Adherence to the Apostolic Succession the Safest Course'. He was followed by J. W. Bowden (*Tract 5*) who wrote on the 'Nature and Constitution of the Church of Christ'. The next three Tracts were by Newman and came out at the end of October, closely followed by two more at the beginning of November. The irrepressible R. H. Froude contributed *Tract 9*, with the title, 'On Shortening Church Services'. Thomas Keble, the brother of John and rector of Bisley, contributed *Tract 12*. Alfred Menzies wrote on the Ember Days, and Benjamin Harrison also contributed two of the four that he eventually produced. This gives an idea of the sense of urgency, and the pace was maintained. By September 1834, a year from the appearance of the first Tracts, the number had grown to 44, which represented nearly half of the final total. Later in the same year the first volume of collected Tracts was published, a practice which continued at intervals until the whole collection was eventually published in six volumes. By the end of 1835 the number had risen to 70. Newman had written 18, Keble had written 7 and E. B. Pusey had done 6. The remainder were shared among a number of authors, none of whom had written more than two or three. Several were reprints or extracts of relevant material from writers of earlier generations, especially the Caroline divines, and were known as *catenae*. They were selected to promote what the Tractarians called 'Church principles'.

Controversy had erupted when E. B. Pusey was persuaded to throw his weight behind the other authors with a Tract. Pusey, had been born in August 1800 and so was a few months older than Newman. He recorded that he 'had the intimacy of my dear and true friend Dr Pusey' from 1823[32] but later said that he had known Pusey well since 1827 or 1828. Pusey had been politically a liberal and had studied theology in Germany. Quite soon he grew to detest such views and tried to suppress the book on German theology that he had written on his return. Pusey married in 1828, but his wife died 11 years later and left him with permanent feeling of remorse and guilt. At the time when he wrote his first Tract, he already had an established academic reputation. He was Regius Professor of Hebrew in the University of Oxford, and was a Canon of Christ Church. He had been appointed to the posts at the comparatively early age of 28, and held them for the rest of his life. In addition, there was a sense of gravitas about Pusey which all recognized: his 'presence always checked Newman's lighter and unrestrained mood', observed Isaac Williams who then added, 'and I was myself silenced by so awful a person'.[33] Newman called him 'the great one', and was correct when he wrote that it was through Pusey 'that the character of the Tracts was changed'. This was because, 'when he gave to us his Tract on Fasting, he put his initials to it'.[34] Newman genuinely admired him for his learning, his industriousness and his devotion. They had walked and talked together, sometimes joined by Isaac Williams. Pusey published *Tract 18* in January 1834 with the title 'Thoughts on the Benefits of the System of Fasting enjoined by our Church'. The manner in which Pusey's first contribution came to be written was somewhat unusual and was described by Isaac Williams:

> He said, smiling to Newman, wrapping his gown round him as he used to do, 'I think you are too hard on the peculiars, as you call them (i.e. the Low Church party); you should conciliate them; I am thinking of writing a letter myself with that purpose.' . . . 'Well!' said Newman, 'suppose you let us have it for one of the Tracts!' 'Oh, no,' said Pusey, 'I will not be one of you!' This was said in a playful manner; and before we parted Newman said, 'Suppose you let us have that letter of yours, which you intend writing, and attach your own name or signature to it. You would then not be mixed up with us, nor in any way responsible for the Tracts!' 'Well,' Pusey said, at last, 'if you will let me do that, I will'.[35]

The idea that someone in Pusey's position could write a signed Tract without becoming identified with the group was naive and a miscalculation. However, Newman, in his *Apologia*, hints that he was overjoyed that Pusey 'showed a disposition to make common cause with us',[36] which may suggest that he was more politically aware than Pusey. *Tract 18* had 28 pages, and was the most substantial document to be published in the series up to that time. Its length established a precedent because later Tracts were not necessarily confined to the format of short pamphlets. H. P. Liddon, who was Pusey's biographer and decades later the leader of the Oxford Movement, explained its length with the observation that 'the writer could not easily express himself other than at length' and went on to point out that number *18* 'covered more ground' and exchanged the character 'of a fugitive composition for that of a theological treatise'. It was also rather obviously contentious, in that the Church of England in the Hanoverian period was not much given to asceticism when Pusey suddenly suggested that fasting had an appropriate and well-attested place within it. Pusey later claimed to be surprised that his argument was not widely accepted: 'I was not prepared for people questioning, even in the abstract, the duty of fasting . . . I assumed the duty to be acknowledged, and thought it only undervalued'.[37] Pusey may have been personally out of touch with the practice of ordinary church-goers. Because the *Tracts for the Times* had begun to attract hostility, it was certain that he would face personal criticism as soon as his Tract on fasting appeared. It was unfortunate for him that he was unwell. Liddon recorded that 'it was, perhaps, inevitable that the Provost of Oriel, who had just been reading Pusey's Tract, should observe that Pusey "must have been fasting too much"'.[38] This amusing, but uncharitable, remark was but one shaft in the volley of criticism that was being fired at the Tracts.

Pusey's Tract was dated St Thomas' Day, 21 December 1833, but Liddon noticed that it was put into circulation at the beginning of the next month. This was shortly after Newman's book on the Arians and just two months before the first volume of his enormously popular *Parochial and Plain Sermons*. Despite these publications, and the other work undertaken by individuals in the group, it was the accession of Pusey to the cause that gave it both identity and status. Newman wrote that he and his friends were 'but individuals'. Dr Pusey, though, 'was, to use the common expression, a host in himself; he was able to give a name, a form and a personality to what was without him a sort of mob.' Consequently, he continued, 'when various parties had met together in order to resist the liberal acts of the Government, we of the Movement took our place by right among them'.[39] Later Newman was to claim that Pusey did not, as such, join the Movement until his treatise on Baptism was produced as *Tracts 57, 58* and *59* in 1835. However, by that date most people not only regarded Pusey as part of the Movement but also as one of its leaders. Indeed, his name was associated ineluctably with it from 1838 when its followers began to be known as 'Puseyites'. Owen Chadwick remarked that that date is the earliest written evidence of the name, but that it has been alleged that it was used three, or even four, years before.[40] The irony of the use of Pusey's name was mentioned by S. L. Ollard. He attributed to its adoption the 'smoothness of its sound . . .

[and] an odd suggestion that there was something funny about it'.[41] 'Dr Pusey's influence was felt at once' said Newman. 'He saw that there ought to be more sobriety, more gravity, more careful pains, more sense of responsibility in the Tracts and in the whole Movement'.[42] Much critical comment continued to be allegations of Romanism. Although it would be disingenuous to say that Newman and his friends were as startled by the charges of Romanism as Pusey claimed to be about the ignorance of fasting, there was some degree in which the allegations did come as a surprise.

Roughly speaking, the criticism of the Tracts which hardened into opposition came from two very different directions. It is convenient to look first at that which, ultimately, was of lesser significance. This was the opposition of liberal theologians, of whom Thomas Arnold is the most representative. He responded with conventional politeness to Pusey's Tract on fasting in a private letter to its author, but soon got down to the issues. 'By the form in which your Tract appears I fear you are lending your cooperation to a party second to none in the tendency of their principle to overthrow the truth of the Gospel.' After that initial onslaught, Arnold offered an emollient observation before returning to the fray, 'your own tract is perfectly free from their intolerance as well as from their folly . . . which has always appeared to me to belong to the Antiquarianism of Christianity – not to its profitable history'. He went on to add that, by the reaction which it produces, 'the admiration of Christian Antiquity seems to me to be the natural parent of Puritanism, which calls all that is ancient Popery'.[43]

Arnold's reference to 'popery' reveals directly the second and more serious charge which was levelled against all the Tracts, not just Pusey's on fasting. Indeed, the earliest criticisms of this sort appeared before Pusey's Tract came out. An evangelical periodical, *The Christian Observer*, and the newspaper *The Record*, launched an attack in December 1833. *The Record* had been founded in 1828 and Newman, then still sympathetic to the evangelicals, had been involved at the beginning. There seems to be a good deal of truth in Arnold's observation that the opponents of the Tracts tended to equate antiquity with Roman Catholicism, for it was to become a common criticism that the Tractarians were trying to establish Roman Catholic doctrines within the Church of England. Indeed, some of the more hysterical of their enemies, such as Walter Walsh in *The Secret History of the Oxford Movement*,[44] claimed that that was precisely their motive. Walsh was probably the most vituperative of all who wrote against the Oxford Movement and his book was published with the support of the

Church Association. This organization was set up in 1865 especially to combat ritualism, which was a spin-off from Tractarianism. Ritualism, the elaboration of ecclesiastical ceremonial, developed slightly later in the nineteenth century and will be considered in Chapter 7. Some opponents even went so far as to claim that the secessions to Roman Catholicism hindered the secret work of those who remained in the Church of England.

At this stage of the Oxford Movement, Newman continued to be strongly opposed to Roman Catholicism. Indeed, his 'advertisement' for the first collected volume of the Tracts was fierce in its attitude to Rome. This was partly due to his evangelical upbringing, but was also an intellectual conviction derived from his studies. Later this was to change, but he was not the only one to feel the attraction of Rome for gradually, with the activities of men such as W. G. Ward, there developed a strong Romanizing section within Tractarianism which damaged both the party and the Church.[45] Newman was later to say that the Romanists 'cut into the original Movement at an angle, fell across its line of thought and then set about turning that line in its own direction'.[46] However, in the early 1830s, accusations and reflections of this sort were still in the future. What Newman, Keble, Pusey and their friends had to contend with were simple allegations that they were disloyal, although this accusation was often combined with the assertion that they were theologically naive rather than sinister. Dean Church's cool prose noted that

> the cry of Romanism was inevitable, and was soon raised [against the Tracts], though there was absolutely nothing in them but had the indisputable sanction of the Prayer Book and of the most authoritative Anglican divines. There was no Romanism in them, nor in anything that showed a tendency to it.

Church's coolness had deserted him towards the end of those two sentences, but he went on to make the interesting observation that some of those persons who were loud in their criticism of the *Tracts for the Times* on grounds of Romanism were themselves not orthodox Anglicans, but were Calvinist or Zwinglian or were 'hopeful and ambitious' liberals in their own theology.[47]

There is no doubt, however, that the Romanist criticisms did strike home. At this time Newman produced two important Tracts to defend himself against the charge. They were numbers *38* and *41* and were a clear statement of moderate Tractarianism.[48] They were in fact one essay and he gave them the title, *The Via Media*. This was the phrase which Newman adapted from the English divines of the seventeenth century and used a good deal. In his mind it defined Anglicanism as a middle way between Rome and dissent. Both Tracts were in the form of a dialogue between 'Clericus', who defends himself against the charge of popery from his interlocutor 'Laicus'. In these Tracts there was the hint of a remark that Newman made in 1864 in his *Apologia*, 'many Anglican divines had been accused of Popery, yet had died in their Anglicanism'.[49] At the time of those Tracts, it is clear that that was Newman's ambition. It was certainly the ambition of Keble and Pusey and, in their cases, was to be fulfilled.

Chapter 3

Controversies

The appointment of Renn Dickson Hampden to succeed Edward Burton as Regius Professor of Divinity at Oxford was the first of a damaging series of disputes. These will be described in this chapter in chronological order, together with an important achievement, the *Library of the Fathers*, which was partly a consequence of the Hampden dispute. By the time of Hampden's appointment to the prestigious professorship, the temperature of theological disagreement in Oxford had risen as a result of the *Tracts for the Times*. When Edward Burton died in January 1836 Newman was immediately anxious that Hampden might be a candidate, although the Tractarians were not alone in opposing Hampden. He would have preferred the professorship to go to some other person, but did hope that Hampden's appointment would bring waverers into the Tractarian fold. Newman told Pusey in a letter written less than a week after Burton died that the ensuing struggle might be an opportunity to 'fight for truth'. There is a hint that some of the chroniclers of the Oxford Movement were embarrassed by the ferocity of the quarrel. Certainly Richard Church seemed to find his loyalty stretched as he described what happened, and even the faithful Liddon came close to hinting that Pusey overreacted to some of the events.

In 1832 Hampden had delivered the Bampton Lectures at Oxford which had raised doubts about his theological orthodoxy. The erudite William Palmer of Worcester College expressed the view of all Hampden's conservative opponents. He felt that the Lectures had a 'tendency [which was] decidedly Rationalistic; that they went to the extent of representing our articles of faith, and our creeds, as based on merely human and uncertain theories'.[1] Hampden reinforced the conservative view that he was unorthodox when he produced a pamphlet in 1834 supporting a scheme to admit Dissenters to the University of Oxford and thus to relax 'subscription' to the Thirty-Nine Articles of Religion. Subscription to the Articles was the device which ensured the domination of the University by the Church. By one of the small ironies of history, Newman was later obliged to read the Thirty-Nine Articles to Hampden when he took his BD degree![2]

It fell to the Prime Minister, Lord Melbourne, to nominate Burton's successor to King William IV. Melbourne needed to consider two factors when making the appointment. The first was political. He needed supporters in positions of influence, and that would have been uppermost in his mind. The second was the theological suitability of the candidate. Archbishop Howley was primarily concerned with the second factor and suggested eight names, but Hampden was not among them. Pusey headed the list; Newman and Keble were fifth and sixth. None of the eight was politically acceptable. So Melbourne wrote to Archbishop Whately in Dublin, who suggested Thomas Arnold and Hampden. The latter's academic career was distinguished. He had been a Fellow of Oriel College before his marriage, and numbered among the Noetics. By the time of his preferment to the Regius Professorship, he was successful as the Principal of St Mary Hall, Oxford, and had been professor of moral philosophy since 1834, a post for which Newman had hoped.[3] Marlborough passed the suggestion of Hampden to Archbishop Howley for consideration[4] who approved, but when it was too late changed his mind. The King allowed Marlborough to go ahead but later also tried unsuccessfully to reverse the decision. Palmer wrote that, 'the University was not long in suspense as to [Burton's] successor. In a few days we were electrified by the intelligence that Dr Hampden was to be appointed to the vacant chair . . . It was like an attempt to force latitudinarian principles on the Church'.[5]

It was important to the Tractarians, and to others who shared the opinion that Hampden was not orthodox, that such a man should not play a major part in the education of undergraduates. This was because the University, with Cambridge, educated virtually all the clergy of the Church of England. William Palmer cited a friend, 'an admirable theologian', in fact H. J. Rose, who had agreed with his own criticisms of the Lectures, and had urged upon him 'the necessity of some protest being made, lest impunity might lead to a repetition of similar attempts against the Articles'.[6] Conservative theologians had been distressed at Hampden's Bampton Lectures, but no objections had been raised at the time. This was fastened upon by his supporters when the quarrel broke out. Hampden was not an inspiring man, he was 'an ugly, solid, dull man with a heavy manner and a harsh voice'.[7] Tom Mozley, who was capable of spiteful remarks, headed a chapter on Hampden, 'The Unreadableness of the Bampton Lectures'.[8] According to Liddon the lectures them-selves were dull, 'They were not very animated compositions; and they were moreover believed to be the echo, if not something more than the echo, of the thoughts of a much more powerful mind than Hampden's – that of Blanco White'.[9] White was an ex-Roman Catho-lic priest who had become an Anglican and had subsequently been at Oriel. He ended his days as a Unitarian. Later Hampden abandoned views that he had taken uncritically from White.[10]

As soon as the news broke that Hampden was to be the new profes-sor, Pusey gave a dinner at which it was agreed to protest against Hampden's appointment because of his unorthodoxy. It was decided to gather a petition signed by the Masters of Arts who happened to be in residence. In the meantime, Newman sat up all night writing a pamphlet, *Elucidations of Dr Hampden's Theological Statements*. Later it was suggested that Newman's title reflected Hampden's obscurity in expressing himself. Newman, though, was trying to prove a more serious charge than obscurity of style. He believed that Hampden could not be trusted with the professorship because he taught heresy. Newman indulged in the clever but dangerous tactic of producing extracts of Hampden's publications, which he prefaced with his own comments, seeking (as he said) 'to assist the judgements of those who are in doubt as to his doctrines, and to explain the earnestness of those who condemn them'.[11] Lord Melbourne, who was not likely to be impartial, dismissed the *Elucidations* as 'abstruse'.

One tactic was to request the Hebdomadal Council of the Univer-sity to call a meeting of the University Convocation with the intention to petition the King, but this time in the name of the University. When Convocation met, an unpleasant moment came at the beginning of the proceedings. As Pusey went to his place he was hissed by some of Hampden's friends who believed that he was motivated by envy at being passed over for the professorship by Lord Melbourne. Pusey was not that sort of man, he simply wanted to prevent the appoint-ment of Hampden. He wrote fruitlessly to Lord Melbourne. The Prime Minister stuck to his decision and also reacted badly to the request from King William IV for reconsideration. Hampden's appointment was formally announced on Wednesday, 17 February

1836, four days after Newman's *Elucidations* had been published, and just under a month after Burton's death. The furore was partially responsible for wider consultations over future Crown appointments[12] and was a factor in the University reforms of the 1850s.

Having failed to prevent the appointment, gradually the momentum began to grow for some way of restricting Hampden's activities within his professorship. The University Convocation decided to exclude Hampden from the committee which nominated select preachers, and proposed that he would not be consulted when the orthodoxy of a sermon was called in question before the Vice-Chancellor. Hampden suffered a further indignity when the Bishop of Exeter granted under-graduates from his diocese an exemption from attending his lectures.

Hampden, probably with a resigned air of determination, got on with preparing his inaugural lecture which was scheduled for 17 March 1836, but he was not allowed to work in peace. Pusey entered the fray on 12 March with a pamphlet designed to supplement Newman's *Elucidations*. Pusey's effort bore the clumsy title, *Dr Hampden's Theological Statements and the Thirty-Nine Articles compared: by a Resident Member of Convocation, with a Preface, and Propositions extracted from his works*. Pusey had some assistance from Benjamin Harrison with the pamphlet. Rather like Newman's, it consisted of quotations, some of them fairly long, from several of Hampden's works, with comment. Pusey arranged the text in parallel columns with the Thirty-Nine Articles for comparison. Forty years later, Liddon loyally tried to justify Pusey's effort, but had to acknowledge that 'the method, however equitable the intention, is liable to be inequitable in effect: the modifying and interpretative force of the context is often lost sight of . . .'.[13]

Hampden's inaugural lecture was evidently an attempt to avoid trouble. Sydney Smith described it, 'A sad affair, this inaugural lecture of Hampden; instead of being like the worldly Hampden, martial and truculent, it is elegiac, precatory and hypocritical'.[14] Even so, Pusey was moved to issue a criticism of the lecture, *Dr Hampden's Past and Present Statements Compared*. Even at this late stage, however, the controversy did not die down completely. Archbishop Whately's chaplain, a Dr Dickinson, issued what he pretended was *A Pastoral Epistle from His Holiness the Pope to some Members of the University of Oxford*. In this pamphlet, Dickinson made out that the Pope approved of the Oxford Movement as pushing in the direction of Rome those who read the *Tracts for the Times*. The Tractarians could have well afforded to ignore this piece of mischief, but Pusey was irritated and went into battle with *An Earnest Remonstrance to the Author of the Pope's Pastoral Letter*. Cast in the terms of a dignified rebuke, he deprecated the use of banter in a serious debate. This point was entirely reasonable, but it indicates that the Tractarians were overreacting. In Pusey's defence it may be that he was stung by an article by a genuine Roman Catholic writer, Nicholas Wiseman the rector of the English College at Rome, in the *Dublin Review*. In it he claimed to be surprised and pleased that the Tractarians were defending orthodox catholic doctrines.[15]

A serious blow was struck from a different quarter on behalf of Hampden. It came from the pen of Thomas Arnold (1795–1842), and was a long article published in the *Edinburgh Review* of April 1836. The title of his article was offensive to the Tractarians, but was evidently composed by the Editor. It was 'The Oxford Malignants and Dr Hampden'. Arnold cannot be entirely excused for the article's title. Close to the beginning, he described the quarrel as 'extraordinary' even when considered in the context of 'party malignity'. Towards the end he described Hampden's opponents as 'malignant fanatics' and compared them to the 'zealots of the circumcision' who persecuted St Paul.[16] Arnold was a famous Headmaster of Rugby School who had been a Fellow of Oriel College between 1815 and 1819. He was the only other clergyman to be considered for the professorship by Melbourne at the time. He felt that he had been victimized by the government, and indeed, the article was later used by newspapers against Arnold's prospects for promotion. Lord Melbourne had tacitly accepted that it would have been politically too dangerous to promote him. The article was the outcome of Arnold's combined unhappiness and anger and it did a great deal of damage to the Tractarian cause. Certainly, his attack on Hampden's opponents was ferocious and intemperate in parts; it even upset his friends.

Arnold had been taken aback by the *Tracts for the Times* and believed that the Oxford Movement embodied a doctrine of the Church which was more appropriate to Roman Catholicism than to the Church of England. He held men such as Pusey, Newman and Keble in high regard personally and shared the nineteenth-century conviction that one could criticize the opinions of others without disagreements deteriorating into personal feuds. It is clear that Arnold was extremely annoyed at the tactics used by the Tractarians. He was particularly angry at the selective manner of Newman's attack in the *Elucidations* and argued, in a letter to an old pupil, 'He [Newman] has in several places omitted sentences in his quotations which give exactly the soft and Christian effect to what, without them, sounds hard and cold'.[17] It was Arnold who said that the author of the pamphlet had used the verb 'to elucidate' to mean 'to misrepresent', and that there 'is no possibility of acquitting the compiler of deliberate dishonesty'.[18]

Arnold's line of argument was clear. He observed that Hampden had been the recipient of notable preferment within Oxford University over a period of years and that some of his promotion had been conferred after the Bampton Lectures to which the Tractarians eventually took exception. Further if Hampden was indeed guilty of heresy, then Oxford University and the Church of England had procedures to follow. This reference to the Church's procedures is not entirely convincing. He thought that the petitions raised by committees were the work of an unofficial and 'an irregular tribunal', which they were, and referred to their 'precious bill of attainder'. He came to see Hampden as the unfortunate victim of attack by others and likened his situation to that of the non-jurors. The non-jurors were churchmen who, after the constitutional upheavals of 1688, found themselves ejected from the ministry of the Church of England because they were unable to accept James II as the lawful king. His biographer makes Arnold sound reasonable, but the parallel with the non-jurors came in a particularly vicious part of the article, and was not sustainable. Arnold's article was an extended review of Hampden's published inaugural lecture and a number of pamphlets, including Newman's *Elucidations*. It was written after the failed attempt to condemn Hampden in Convocation. He expressed the fear that the attack in Convocation would soon be renewed. This is exactly what happened in the month that the article appeared, and the unfortunate Hampden did have to endure censure.

But the quarrel did not vanish from the ecclesiastical scene when Hampden was installed, yet inhibited, as Regius Professor. In 1847, with a different Prime Minister, Lord John Russell, he was made Bishop of Hereford. The opposition re-ignited, but the Anglo-Catholics were still weak after the debacle of 1845. Keble felt strongly and was probably behind a protest which was made at the episcopal confirmation ceremony in Bow church. Pusey took little part in the protest, although he wrote to Harrison in the hope that he might be able to exert influence on the Archbishop of Canterbury, but to no avail. Other protests were made, no less than 13 bishops presented an address of remonstrance to Russell. As in the earlier controversy, the nomination went ahead. Hampden was allowed to end his days in Herefordshire obscurity more than 20 years later. The imputation that he was a heretic fell away as he conscientiously administered his diocese. He abandoned 'those dubious opinions that he had received uncritically from Blanco White'. They had 'never been an integral part of his philosophy' and when he died in April 1868, he was 'revered and honoured as one of the most conservative bishops of . . . the bench'.[19]

The effect on the Oxford Movement of the controversy over Hampden's professorship was not good. The battle had been lost. The Tractarians had made an unwise choice of battleground for Newman's 'fight for truth'. Further, it was an overreaction which damaged the Tractarians by emphasizing the conservative nature of their theology while also playing into the hands of opponents who were anxious to condemn them as a romanizing influence within the Church of England. On the positive side, it served to bring to the attention of many a movement which was trying to highlight the catholic nature of the Church of England's heritage. In addition, Newman's reputation was enhanced when he was acknowledged as supporting orthodoxy against heresy, but he had chosen the wrong battleground and the Tractarians had gained more enemies. On balance, the verdict must be that the Hampden controversy was harmful to the Movement, not least because the Tractarians took the blame for all the opposition. This was not entirely fair, as other conservative Churchmen had also deplored Hampden's theology.

An important and worthwhile literary consequence of the Hampden row for the Tractarians was the decision to produce the *Library of the Fathers*.[20] This was a series of English translations of selected writings of the 'Early Fathers', who were the formative theologians of the early centuries of Christianity. Pusey and Newman thought it desirable that the study of the works of the Fathers should be more widespread among members of the Church of England, particularly the clergy. It was clear to them that there was much to be said for providing translations of the actual texts rather than merely selections or extracts such as the *catenae* in the *Tracts* series. The editors knew that the writings of the Fathers had a substantial value of their own. As spiritual reading, they gave their readers something to think about, and helped to preserve a broader vision. The relevant texts were often difficult to locate, not easily accessible to those who were not expert in the original Latin or Greek. In addition, they were often only available in cumbersome and expensive 'folio' volumes, and few potential readers had access to theological libraries. They hoped that the series would carry forward at a more profound level what they had started with the *Tracts for the Times*.

The idea took shape in late August 1836, when Pusey and Newman stayed at the house of a mutual friend, a few miles from Oxford. Pusey drafted a letter that he submitted to Newman before sending it to nearly a dozen others. Later it was to have a wider circulation. At this very early stage, Keble was not involved, but Pusey wrote to him in September and told him that they wanted him to be a joint editor, making it 'a treble cord'.[21] Keble was proud to be associated with the project. Characteristically, he said he was 'conscious of my knowledge of the Catholic Fathers being too limited by far to justify such a step had I been [able] to choose for myself'.[22] At different times, both of the other men were to claim their ignorance, but the production of the series of volumes was to prove otherwise. After Keble was committed to sharing the editorship, an approach was made to Archbishop Howley for support. He agreed to become a Patron of the project and sent a favourable reply on 11 October 1836. Keble saw Howley when the latter visited Hursley Park, and they had a satisfactory conversation. It was Howley who suggested that each volume should have a preface, supplied by one of the editors. Pusey secured the support of Bishop Blomfield of London. The Bishop of Oxford declared that he found the proposal for the Library agreeable. With what amounted to a good deal of encouragement, Pusey went ahead with the production of a 'prospectus'. It was planned to publish it in the October editions of both *The British Critic* and the *British Magazine*.

The Library made available the texts which had established catholic doctrines, such as the apostolic succession, the divine origin of the Church and the true nature of the sacraments. The Church of England claimed the Fathers as part of its neglected heritage. The works of the Fathers had been declared, in a Canon of Convocation in 1571, to be authoritative for the Church of England. Pusey quoted the relevant passage, the clergy 'shall be careful never to teach anything from the pulpit to be religiously held and believed by the people, but what is agreeable to the doctrine of the Old and New Testament, and collected out of that same doctrine by the Catholic Fathers and ancient Bishops'.[23] It was with some delight that Pusey saw that the same Canon enforced subscription to the Thirty-Nine Articles of Religion. Pusey claimed that making the texts of the Fathers accessible helped to refute the arguments of men such as Hampden. Pusey wrote that the Fathers, 'I think . . . have altogether a deeper way of viewing things than moderns, deeper and truer thoughts . . .'.[24] Another advantage was that by promoting the writings of the early Fathers as part of the heritage of the Church of England, the editors were implicitly answering those churchmen who wrongly regarded them as the intellectual property of Roman Catholicism.

Saints Augustine, Athanasius and Chrysostom, together with Cyprian, Cyril and Ambrose are typical of the Fathers selected and, simply listed, give a flavour of the series as a whole. It would be a mistake to assume that Pusey, Newman and Keble believed the Fathers to be a monochrome collection of theologians. They knew the writings well, despite their protestations of personal ignorance, and recognized the objection that there were things in the Fathers that were uncongenial to the Tractarians. Another objection voiced the old-fashioned Puritan opinion that the Fathers were merely 'fallible men' and, as a consequence, should not have particular weight given to their authority. Pusey dealt with the latter aspect directly, and implicitly with the first. The Church's appeal, he wrote, is 'not to the Fathers individually, or as individuals, but as witnesses; not to this or that Father, but to the whole body, and agreement of Catholic Fathers and ancient Bishops'.[25]

The scheme has been described in some detail because of its importance. It suggests also that there were likely to be problems in carrying it out. The first difficulty was the obvious one of selecting particular writers and works for translation. The editors wanted to keep away from what they called 'narrowness', or partisan selectiveness in the choice of material, but were driven by the desire to emphasize catholicity. The overriding motive seems to have been to demonstrate, in Liddon's words, that 'the Fathers attest the existence of Catholic agreement in a great body of truth in days when the Church of Christ was still visibly one, and still spoke one language'.[26] In this way they could serve as a 'safeguard against modern errors'. As an Appendix to his chapter on the *Library of the Fathers* in his biography of Pusey, Liddon provided a list of all the Fathers translated. He included sufficient information to identify each piece of every selected Father's work, together with the name of the translator, the date when the book appeared and also the name of the author of each preface.[27] With regard to the prefaces, in addition to the labours of the three editors, a great deal of work was done by Charles Marriott. He was a precise and conscientious scholar who shouldered the burden of editorship after Newman's secession, and was worn down by it.

More than 20 translators worked on the series between 1838 and 1885. One who assisted was Pusey's wife, Maria. She was competent in Latin as well as two modern languages, and the former was useful when she worked for her husband on St Augustine's *Confessions* and later on St Cyprian. A difficulty lay in the nature of the work of translation. The particular problem was whether scholars would be expected to follow Pusey's rigidity of style which sacrificed idiom in favour of an exact rendering of the original author. This rigidity had unfavourably affected translations done by Pusey in the past, but it seems to have prevailed initially. It was this policy that led to Tom Mozley's sharp comment, 'perhaps it is impossible to translate a Christian Father so as to make him pleasant reading, or even to satisfy the requirements of common sense'.[28] A practical matter was whether the translators should be paid, and Newman was eventually convinced that they should. Pusey was not convinced, and always expected that he and the others should do their work for nothing. Eventually he offered to put up £1,000 of his own money to cover the cost of publication. Remarkably the publisher, Rivingtons, ignored this generous offer and pressed ahead with their own plan for a subscription list. Just before the first volume appeared, his own edition of the *Confessions of St Augustine*, Pusey was alarmed at the small number of subscribers. This anxiety was misplaced in the long run as it eventually grew to more than 3,700.[29]

The plan was to produce four volumes of the Library each year, but this ambitious goal was not achieved until 1843, when five were published, but even then it was not sustained. Pusey's translation of the *Confessions of St Augustine* did not appear until August 1838, almost two years after the inception of the scheme. Richard Church produced the second volume in the series, a translation of the *Catechetical Lectures* of St Cyril of Jerusalem, later in 1838, and two other volumes, the work of other translators, appeared in 1839. The project continued steadily, although much more slowly than the editors had hoped. 1846, the year after Newman left the Church of England, did not see any volume, but the series continued until 1885. No fewer than 48 volumes eventually appeared, spread over a period of 47 years from the publication of Pusey's *St Augustine*. Their appeal was wider than simply to the partisan followers of the Anglo-Catholics. The series was acknowledged to have been a steadying influence at a time of upheaval and turmoil in the Church of England. The books were to sustain that influence for nearly half a century. The *Library of the Fathers* helped the followers of the Oxford

Movement to feel that the ancient Church supported the position they had taken.

A few months before the *Library of the Fathers* was suggested, the Tractarian Movement lost a potentially great leader. Hurrell Froude was struck down by 'consumption', just before his thirty-third birthday. He died on 28 February 1836 in the house in which he had been born. Tom Mozley ranked him with Newman as vying for the role of the 'master spirit of this movement'.[30] Froude's death at such an early age was keenly felt by his friends. His younger brother J. A. Froude, who was eventually very unsympathetic to the views of the Tractarians, acknowledged that Hurrell Froude was 'gifted, brilliant and enthusiastic'.[31] Froude had shared the desire of Keble and Newman to fight for the rights and privileges of the Church of England when in 1833 they appeared to be under threat. Eventually he was the author of two *Tracts for the Times*, numbers 9 and 59, the latter being a short discussion on 'The Position of the Church of Christ in England, relatively to the State and the Nation'. It came out in April 1835, after his return from the West Indies, to which he had retreated for health reasons in November 1834. His passing proved to be a disaster for the Oxford Movement and his friends felt his loss acutely. Froude's father gave Newman his son's journals, sermons and letters. He invited Newman to publish whatever he thought appropriate of his son's papers, and he promised to pay the bill. The cause of the calamity was a lack of practical wisdom in the selection of material for publication in what came to be called *The Remains of the late Reverend Richard Hurrell Froude*.

Hurrell Froude had been almost born a Tory. He was the eldest son of Archdeacon Robert Froude of Totnes in Devonshire. His father was a classic example of the old 'high and dry' churchmanship, a magistrate and a landowner in his own right. Hurrell Froude left Eton and became an undergraduate at Oriel College in 1821. He arrived with a letter of introduction to John Keble and the relationship soon developed from that of undergraduate and don into a fast friendship. This was cemented when Froude was one of three undergraduates whom Keble invited to a vacation 'reading party'. The other members of the group were Robert Wilberforce and Isaac Williams and all three young men admired Keble's virtue, holiness and air of reserve. Keble checked some aspects of Froude's ebullient and forceful character, but he was also influenced by his younger friend. Keble allowed Froude, who always pushed his arguments hard and to their logical conclusion, to alter some of his theological opinions.

Froude prospered intellectually in the atmosphere of Oriel College and was elected to a Fellowship in 1826. His election brought him into direct contact with Newman in the Senior Common Room. In the first volume of the *Remains* is included a remark which Froude made 'with his death in prospect'. He said, 'Do you know the story of the murderer who had done one good thing in his life? Well, if I were ever asked what good deed I have ever done, I should say I had brought Keble and Newman to understand each other.'[32] Froude certainly believed this and his expression of the conviction was touching. Newman was much attracted to Froude's sharp wit, logical mind and obvious intellectual ability and, he said, they enjoyed 'the closest and most affectionate friendship' from 1829.[33] Consequently Newman was a natural choice to accompany Froude and his father on the Mediterranean trip. Shortly after Hurrell Froude's death his father invited Newman to select one of his late son's books as a keepsake. After much indecision, Newman chose Froude's Roman Breviary. He used it for many years, beginning while still an Anglican. His ultimately unsuccessful plans to translate the Breviary into English fuelled the accusations of 'popery'.

Having been astonished and captivated by what he read in Froude's papers, Newman nevertheless had some reservations and consulted Keble. Together, they allowed their fascination to override sober judgement and went ahead with publication. The decision reflects an understandable reverence for a dead friend's memory and may also indicate the posthumous force of Froude's personality. The editorship of Froude's collected works was a task which they decided to share and has generally been taken as illustrating their mutual understanding. However, the publication of the collection was a tactical disaster which suggests that, fundamentally, the two did not understand each other. If, as seems likely, the initiative had come from Newman, who had been the recipient of the papers, the lack of mutual understanding is more acute. This was revealed in the conviction shared by Keble's brother, Tom, and sister, Elizabeth, that John Keble was 'too much inclined to let Newman have matters all his own way'.[34] The editors were convinced that Froude's devotion and personal holiness would speak for itself and enhance the reputation of the movement. This was strange in view of Keble's normal reserve and his advice to 'put all one's confessions in the fire'.[35] Keble's first biographer, J. T. Coleridge, recorded that the lengthy Preface to the first volume of Froude's *Remains* was written by Keble with some input from Newman. If that is so, and

Newman merely added minor elements, it is clear that both men had reservations.

After some biographical material, the Preface moved to an apology for the 'very magnitude of the collection'. At the time of writing Keble and Newman expected to publish two volumes, eventually they produced four, although it was the first volume which was the most contentious. The apology continued 'as though authority were being claimed in a preposterous way, for the opinions of one undistinguished either by station or by known literary eminence'.[36] Later came the observation that

> the publication of a private journal and private letters is a curious thing . . . painful, nay revolting, to expose to the common gaze papers only intended for a single correspondent; and it seems little less than sacrilege to bring out the solitary memoranda of one endeavouring to feel, and to be, as much as possible alone with his God.[37]

Keble's unease, or perhaps it was Newman's, was clearly close to the surface with the expression of such sentiments. The editors excused themselves, however, by emphasizing the remarkable nature of Froude's personality. They believed that his theological opinions were highly important in their own right. They were also convinced that Froude's observations were given a greater authority because he lived for so long under the shadow of death. Despite these convictions, the Preface is redolent with the editors' unease, and it may even have helped to provoke the storm of criticism which the book attracted.

The first two volumes of Froude's *Remains*, together with the unfortunate Preface, appeared in March 1838. Volume 1 began with extracts from his private journal from 1823. It was the record of an overscrupulous young man. It opened with trivial notes of self-criticism about his time wasting. He noted that he had talked to others about religious observance, but felt that he was too severe because of his own 'bad actions and feelings'. Froude resolved not to argue with his father and recorded his distress at failing to keep his resolution. It was not the sort of material to make the mind of a reader well disposed to the author, and his self-criticism about eating too much and playing cards tends to increase the reader's exasperation. Keble and Newman had as their motive the desire to present to their own time an example of noble austerity. Heroic sanctity, they were trying to show, was a factor in the spiritual life of the Church of England and definitely to be found in the Movement which they had started.

Froude's papers revealed traces of morbidity and introspection. Readers encountered a man who slept on the floor and recorded his reluctance to do so.[38] There were other aspects of self-mortification, additional austerity and self-denial; for example, 'no dinner but a little bread'.[39] Mixed in with these sentiments he accused himself of 'pleasure' at the shortcomings of others and worried about his debts. Indeed, Archdeacon Froude, whilst admitting that the 'strict scrutiny . . . unsparing severity . . . and earnest endeavours' of his son were 'certainly most interesting features of his character, [such elements] possibly might have been better kept out of sight'.[40]

Those who penetrated deeper into the book found more specific matters for concern. Froude revealed a 'romantic vision of the mediaeval Church'[41] and consequently was critical of the Reformation. This was one of the areas in which he had influenced Keble, who also had become more critical of the Reformation and the Reformers. Froude's character had an element of the gadfly about it, so his language was unmeasured and sometimes stinging. In a letter to a friend who is not named, he wrote in 1834, 'You will be shocked at my avowal, that I am every day becoming a less and less loyal son of the Reformation'.[42] He continued with the suggestion that, where appropriate, 'we should conform our practices to those of the Church which has preserved its traditionary [*sic*] practices unbroken'.[43] Such a statement was just the sort of thing that opponents of the Oxford Movement suspected. His father, in the letter which has already been quoted, had written, 'I daresay he was often tempted to use stronger expressions on that subject [the Reformation] than his real feelings warranted'.[44]

In a similar vein, his practical suggestion for the Church to operate pastorally in 'great towns' through the ministry of 'colleges of unmarried priests'[45] was also interpreted as barely concealed Roman Catholicism. From about the same time there came a statement by Froude that 'Since I have been at home, I have been doing what I can to proselytize in an underhand way'.[46] To the opponents of the Oxford Movement, this seemed to confirm beyond all reasonable doubt that he had been dishonest and that his editors had foolishly revealed their own practice by publishing Froude's. It did not matter that Froude was also rude about Roman Catholicism, nor that the Preface had been careful to include explanation and defence along with a denial that Froude's opinions were 'popery'. Newman and Keble 'read the book in the correcting light of friendship while the world judged Froude by the book'.[47]

Dean Church said 'the world was shocked'[48] by the publication of Froude's *Remains*. It alienated many old-fashioned High Churchmen. One of them was Joshua Watson, who was disturbed by the book and already suspicious of the Tractarians. To the enemies of the Oxford Movement, the book lent itself to dissection. Controversialists set to work 'culling choice phrases and sentences and epithets surprisingly at variance with conventional and popular estimates'. Richard Church noted that friends of Froude and of the movement were hurt and upset, whereas foes 'could not hold their overflowing exultation at such a disclosure of the spirit of the movement'. The press was already hostile to the Oxford Movement, and Froude's *Remains* was a golden opportunity for an attack. The fear of incipient Roman Catholicism within the Church of England had been rising with the publication of the *Tracts for the Times* and the development of a recognizable Romanizing element among the followers of the Tractarians. That fear received a fillip from the *Remains* and critics continued to wonder about the possibility of dishonesty.

In Oxford a divinity professor preached a University Sermon from Newman's own pulpit in St Mary's Church and condemned Froude and his *Remains* along with his editors. Bishop Bagot of Oxford, who had shown a cautiously tolerant attitude earlier to the *Tracts for the Times*, was critical. Newman replied to both, and made matters worse, with his undeniable skill in controversy. Newman and Keble hoped that the *Remains* would help in the acceptance of the views of the Tractarians. In a sense, they saw Froude as the Movement's first martyr and they commended what, in the preface, they had called 'these fragments' because their author had always sought to offer 'a word in season'. They commended them in the hope that Froude ' "being dead" . . . may "yet speak" . . . [and] may still have the privilege of awakening some of her [the Church's] members to truer and more awful thoughts than they now have . . .'.[49] It was a serious miscalculation. Pusey was disturbed and it is interesting to note that Liddon's great biography of Pusey mentions Froude's *Remains* only in the briefest manner when references to it cannot be avoided.

Eventually the furore over the *Remains* died away, but another defeat was in store. The key figure in the next round was the Reverend Charles Pourtales Golightly (1807–85), a man of independent means and a former Oriel pupil of Newman who had once considered him as a possible curate. Golightly was, by this time, an outspoken opponent of the Tracts and their authors. He called a meeting at his home to stir up opposition to the editors of Froude's *Remains*. The group hit upon the ingenious idea of raising subscriptions to commemorate the key figures of the English Reformation. Cranmer, Ridley and Latimer had all been burned at the stake in Oxford. Golightly and his friends thus made the deaths of the sixteenth-century Oxford martyrs a nineteenth-century party issue. There was some regret among the Tractarians and others that, as Benjamin Harrison shrewdly and wittily put it, 'the martyrs were to be made bones of contention in Oxford'. The scheme was to build a church in their memory, or to erect a memorial cross. It was a source of Tractarian regret that the site of the martyrs' suffering had not been properly marked from early days, as this would have prevented Golightly from raising the matter. Golightly's trap was a simple one. Individuals would be invited to give money for the project as a practical demonstration of their loyalty to the memory of the martyrs. Failure to subscribe would be construed as a repudiation of the doctrines and principles for which the three men had gone to the stake. Golightly and his friends knew, of course, that Keble and Newman would find themselves in the dilemma of denying either their loyalty to the dead Froude or to the martyred Reformers.

Newman thought that the plan was an act of spite. In a letter he went to the heart of the dispute. The idea was 'to force your humble servant to subscribe to it *or* not'.[50] Pusey, who had not shared in the editorship of the *Remains*, had not gone so far as Newman, Keble and Froude in rejecting the Reformers. He was personally willing to acknowledge the 'blessings of the Reformation', but was caught up in the issue by implication. It was characteristic of him to get involved. He knew that it was a 'hit' against Keble and Newman. It was some time before he decided against subscribing. Pusey's decision had two aspects. First, his loyalty to his friends. Second, a theological recognition that one of the great advantages of the Church of England was 'that we had no human founder: we were not identified with men, or any set of men; it was God's mercy that we had so little of human influence'.[51] He had made this very point some years earlier in *Tract 69*. Later in a letter to Keble written in January 1839, he repeated it. It was a 'blessing' that the Church of England did not look to a Zwingli or a Calvin or a Luther. This lack of an identifiable confessor or founder meant that the Church of England did not have a starting-point. This was important in the thinking of men such as Pusey. It demonstrated, as he wrote to Bishop Bagot, that the Church of England was not 'a new Church of the Reformation' although he admitted this was the 'vulgar impression'. Rather it was 'the old [Church] one purified'.

Whilst the Tractarians were trying to deal with the cleverly posed dilemma, Golightly's plans to build a church were also running into trouble. The appeal had not raised sufficient money. It struck the Tractarians that Oxford was not showing as much enthusiasm for the martyred Reformers as Golightly had expected. Acidly, Newman wondered if they would have to be 'contented with busts in the Bodleian [Library]'.[52] The proposers of the memorial were in the invidious position of having insufficient money pledged for a church, and rather less if the memorial was to be simply a memorial cross. The erection of a cross was pursued as an alternative, so long as it could be erected on the site of the fires. Pusey was definitely sympathetic to this idea because, he said, it was not 'respectful' for carts and other vehicles 'to drive over the place where they yielded up their souls'.[53] In the end, no subscriptions came from Newman, Keble or Pusey. A cross was erected, several years later, in 1842. It was round the corner from the site of the fires. The surplus money was used to add a 'martyrs' aisle' to the adjacent parish church of St Mary Magdalene. Golightly's intention to embarrass Newman, Keble and Pusey had been only partly successful, but the Oxford Movement had suffered several setbacks. Worse was to follow.

Chapter 4

The End of the Tracts

Pusey's substantial work on baptism had removed any lingering doubts about the theological seriousness of the *Tracts for the Times*. Further Tracts were published and were a mixture of sermons, specially written material and what the editors called *catenae*. Despite their polemical tone, and the fact that they were now becoming substantial treatises, the series did not attract serious controversy until Isaac Williams wrote *Tract 80* in 1837. W. J. Conybeare, writing in the *Edinburgh Review* in October 1853, provided an explanation. He thought that the earlier Tracts contained 'a *bona fide* attempt to base the creed of the Church strictly upon Anglican tradition', but he was highly critical of later developments which he thought to be Romanism.[1]

Williams was not in any sense a 'Romanist', but he was the unlucky creator of a theological storm. We are fortunate to have his own description of events. He wrote an autobiography, but its value is limited because of his great personal modesty. It was a private composition for his children because he felt that they would be 'glad to know something of the history' of his life. 'Parts of it', he continued, had 'been spent among persons and circumstances in themselves of some interest and moment, and such as must have some effect on the future character and history of the Church in this country.' Later, the work was published by his brother-in-law, the Venerable Sir George Prevost.

Williams' Tract had as its title, 'On Reserve in Communicating Religious Knowledge', which had been suggested by Newman. In Williams' opinion, the title was as much responsible for the controversy as were the actual contents of the essay. However, he retained the title when in 1840 he wrote a supplementary Tract, 87, 'in explanation' and to meet 'all reasonable objections excepting those of the Low Church'.[2] The origin of *Tract 80* was a paper Williams had been writing on the gospel commentaries compiled by Origen, a third-century scholar. There he had noticed 'how much he alluded to a mysterious holding back of sacred truth, such as I had always been struck with in the conduct of the Kebles'.[3] He showed his work to John Keble, who suggested that he should offer it to the Friday evening discussion meetings which Pusey had instigated in his house after his wife's death. These were a way of developing a common mind among the followers of the Tractarians at a time when they 'were swelling into a large party'.[4] The decision to publish it as a *Tract for the Times* was made by the author in discussion with Pusey and Newman, probably on the evening of its delivery.

The concept which Williams found in Origen was the ancient catholic doctrine of the *Disciplina Arcani*, or 'discipline of the secret'. This was a conscious endeavour in the early Church, when faced with persecution, to conceal the intimate details of the faith from uninformed newcomers and from potentially hostile non-members. It was a doctrinal stance which was open to misinterpretation as well as misunderstanding when recollected within nineteenth-century Anglicanism. It led to hostility and created, within some elements of Anglo-Catholicism, a sense of introspection which lingered for many years. Nevertheless, the concept of reserve had its place in Church history. Williams' opponents were wrong to dismiss it as a form of Tractarian obscurantism and even more in error to assume that 'reserve' really meant a secret Romanist plot.

Remarkably, there were hints of the doctrine of reserve in Hurrell Froude's *Remains*, which Newman and Keble were editing at the time of the controversy over Williams' Tract. By contrast, Froude himself had said to Isaac Williams, 'Isaac, we must make a row in the world . . . Church principles forced on the people's notice must work for good . . . We must try . . .'.[5] He could not have expected that Williams would contribute much to the row, for Williams was a quiet, peace-loving man who would, in the normal course of events, never have become a controversialist. It is likely that Froude's words were little more than idle 'thinking aloud' in his friend's presence. They had become friends in the long vacation of 1823 on John Keble's reading party. Prior to that summer Williams had no great interest in theology. As a boy and undergraduate he said he had thought in Latin, so it was unremarkable that such a man won an undergraduate prize for Latin verse. What made it significant was that Keble called on him in his rooms and 'offered his help in criticizing the poem and polishing it for printing'.[6]

Keble, when he got to know Williams, had revised his plans for the reading party and invited him to join the group.

'It was this very trivial accident, this short walk of a few yards, and a few words spoken', said Williams in reference to Keble's visit and invitation, 'which was the turning point of my life. If a merciful God had miraculously interposed to arrest my course, I could not have had a stronger assurance of His presence than I always had in looking back to that day'.[7] Keble influenced Williams permanently. He was 10 years younger than Keble, and a year older than Froude, but more like the former in temperament. The attractiveness of Keble's style and manner was important to Williams because it reflected precisely his own developing personality. His younger contemporary, R. W. Church, wrote of his 'reverence' of mind, his 'humility, self-restraint and self-abasement'.

Williams did not expect his Tract to cause any excitement or violent disagreement. The controversy would have pleased Froude, but he had died in 1836, the year before it came out. Williams said at the beginning of *Tract 80*:

> The object of the present inquiry is to ascertain, whether there is not in God's dealings with mankind, a very remarkable holding back of sacred and important truths, as if the knowledge of them were injurious to persons unworthy of them. And, if this be the case, it will lead to some important practical reflections.[8]

He was convinced that Scripture itself contains the principle of reserve. A considerable amount of *Tract 80* is given over to demonstrations of the veiled nature of the Bible. Williams gave the first 30 'hidden' years of Christ's earthly life as a significant example of how the theory of 'reserve' is in accordance with the biblical witness. In fact he took the argument further back, and in a footnote gave an unidentified reference to Chrysostom as having cited the view of the 'the Fathers' that 'our Saviour's being born a virgin, was perhaps one of the secret things not first made known to the Jews'. Similarly, the Lord's crucifixion was the time 'when his divinity was most shrouded'. The resurrection itself, 'seems in such a striking manner to have been kept back, if I may so speak, from the gaze of the multitude, from the broad light of the common day'.[9] Having drawn briefly from the general pattern of the life of Christ, Williams later went on to argue from particular instances of reserve in the teaching of Christ, such as the parables, and also his miracles. Actions by Christ and incidents within his life were accorded separate consideration. Williams claimed that they demonstrated 'the same secret mode of teaching'. He then analysed the way in which the Lord was spoken about by others, and also the way in which he spoke of himself, and finally concluded, 'The whole history of this, the ALMIGHTY'S mode of revealing Himself, is the circumstance which has been matter of offence to the unbeliever, asking for a sign.'[10]

Williams occasionally allowed himself to be polemical. He made small but pointed criticisms of Roman Catholicism which, he claimed, demonstrated God's reserve through permitting error. He was critical of Protestantism in the same way.

The precise relevance of these observations to the concept of reserve was made clear in part of the Tract which Williams headed, 'That God punishes with blindness those who approach sacred truths with a speculative mind'. Knowledge of spiritual truths is to be gained by way of what he called 'practical obedience'. Bishops Andrewes, Wilson, and Butler were classical Anglicans whom he called upon to support the assertions which he made in this context. His conclusions are in accordance with that eschewing of originality which is to be found in the writings of Keble and Pusey and in the latter's disciple, H. P. Liddon. However determined the Tractarians were to avoid anything approaching originality, they often failed to recognize that their rediscovery and representation of ancient truths was a novelty to many of their contemporaries. It was this fact which caused Williams so much trouble with his two Tracts. Many of his readers were shocked. *Tract 80* seemed to confirm their fears that the Tractarians were secret Romanists. Williams' doctrine of reserve was accused of being an intellectual shield which allowed Roman Catholicism to do its work within the Church of England under the guise of devotion, caution and discretion. Because of the volatile atmosphere, Williams' theory, although in fact straightforward, was a dangerous one to promote under the Tractarian banner at that time. Any suggestion that the Oxford men were not entirely open in their teaching offered hostages to fortune. Williams' own character was such that he found reticence congenial, but such were the current circumstances that hints of secrecy and reluctance to be forthcoming about religious teaching fuelled the blaze kindled by the appearance of the Tracts. Keble only added to the controversy when, in *Tract 89*, he included a defence of the doctrine of reserve.

As the *Tracts for the Times* became the focus of contention, so Newman began to feel the attraction of Roman Catholicism, despite his earlier fierce denunciations of it. At the same time there developed what Dean Church called a 'strong Romanizing section in the Tractarian party'. This section was obviously damaging to the Tractarians and dangerous for the Church. Eventually, Newman reached the conclusion that he should write a Tract about 'certain passages' in the Thirty-Nine Articles of Religion. His motive was the hope of settling the minds of the 'Romanizing section', and also of settling his own.

There were two principal reasons for the controversy that developed. The first was the fear of 'Romanism', which was a deep-seated prejudice within English life. The Thirty-Nine Articles of Religion were thought to combat it and to define English Protestantism, although they were less Protestant in doctrine than many at the time wished to believe.[11] The second reason for the great quarrel was the specific situation within Oxford University, which until 1854 was only open to members of the Church of England. All who wished to become members of the University were obliged to subscribe to the Articles.

Another reason was his desire to go into print in opposition to R. D. Hampden and those who would have relaxed subscription to the Articles in a liberal direction. The celebrated *Tract 90* was dated 25 January 1841. Writing anonymously, Newman set out to demonstrate how the Articles could be interpreted in a catholic (but still non-Roman) sense. Newman provided a useful introduction to the Tract, but it is difficult for the reader of a later generation to read it without feeling that it was the work of an already unsettled mind. At the end of *Tract 90*, Newman returned to the underlying anxiety. He feared, he said, that some would think the 'the tenor of the above explanations is anti-Protestant'. He preferred to think that this was not the case. However, 'it is a *duty* . . . to take our reformed confessions in the most Catholic sense they will admit'.[12] He argued that his interpretation of the Thirty-Nine Articles would 'bring them into harmony with the Prayer Book'. This was consistent with his assertion that the Articles 'are evidently framed on the principle of leaving open large questions'[13] and in such a way as to include those who 'did not go so far in Protestantism' as the original compilers.[14] Dean Church, at the start of his discussion of *Tract 90*, pointed out that 'the class of arguments which especially laid hold of Mr Newman's mind did not tell upon' the other Oxford leaders. They were 'quite unaffected by the disquieting apprehensions which were beginning to beset Mr Newman'.[15]

In *Tract 90* Newman did not deal with all the Thirty-Nine Articles, but only with 14. There was no need to do more, for the others were not considered by him to need a catholic interpretation. He devoted most space to Article 22, 'Purgatory, Pardons, Images, Relics, Invocations of the Saints'. His manner of dealing with it provides a good example of how he worked. He began by saying something positive. He commented that it was the 'Romish' doctrines that were specifically condemned. He then argued, that the primitive doctrines which did exist are not condemned, 'whatever their merits'. The use of this phrase was his acknowledgement that legitimate differences of opinion existed in antiquity. With this Article he then turned, as was his customary practice in *Tract 90*, to quotations from the *Book of Homilies*[16] which he used to expand and develop his argument. Gradually, in each case, Newman worked to the conclusion that he had in mind. With Article 22, this was complicated by the fact that it dealt with a number of contentious doctrines, but he repeated his early assertion that the Article did not condemn primitive versions of the doctrines.

More than once in the Tract, Newman pointed out that the classical doctrine of the Roman Catholic Church, as defined at the Council of Trent (1545–63), was not under attack in the Articles, because they were compiled before the Council completed its deliberations. Keble privately made a specific criticism of this point. He observed that the Council of Trent had adopted the earlier definitions of purgatory compiled by the Schoolmen.[17] This meant that, in Keble's view, it was disingenuous of Newman simply to argue that the Council of Trent postdated the Thirty-Nine Articles. Keble also thought that Newman's later revision of the Tract also did not really deal with the point. It was a real weakness in Newman's argument.

It is not difficult to see why *Tract 90* raised a storm of controversy first within Oxford University and later throughout the Church of England. Joshua Watson, who more-or-less typified the laity of the old-fashioned form of High Churchmanship, did not like *Tract 90*. Along with Froude's *Remains*, Newman's Tract left him feeling that Tractarianism was untrustworthy. Even so, he did not become an opponent of the Movement. Others did, and R. W. Church said that the Tract was met 'not with argument, but with panic and wrath'.[18] The controversy hardened and the proceedings about *Tract 90* became a 'declaration of war on the part of the Oxford authorities against the Tractarian party. The suspicions, alarms, antipathies, jealousies, which had long been smouldering among those in power, had at last taken shape in a definite act'.[19]

The first protest came in the form of a letter signed by four senior tutors, although they were by no means the Tract's only opponents. They were A. C. Tait of Balliol College and a future Archbishop of Canterbury; John Griffiths of Wadham College; H. B. Wilson of St John's College and T. T. Churton of Brasenose College, 'two Latitudinarians and two Evangelicals', said Pusey.[20] The theological heavyweights were Tait and Churton. Predictably, a collaborator was C. P. Golightly. Newman was convinced that he 'was the sole conductor of the whole matter'.[21] He bought many copies of the Tract and posted one to each diocesan bishop, inviting them to condemn it.

Tait was worried that the Tracts would lead undergraduates towards Roman Catholicism. His biographers preserved his own description of his motive:

> if young men lose their confidence in that branch of the Church of Christ of which they are members, and have their attention forced to curious questions that seem only to minister strife, there seems no telling to what extent their whole religious character may be affected.[22]

He was also critical of the logic behind the views of Newman and his friends. A friend of Tait's was quoted by his biographers, to his 'downright common sense the whole movement seemed nonsense, or at least the madness of incipient Popery'.[23] It was the irrepressible W. G. Ward who drew *Tract 90* to Tait's attention. Tait 'was sitting quietly in his rooms in Balliol on Saturday morning, February 27, 1841, when Ward burst excitedly in. "Here", he cried, "is something worth reading!" and he threw down a pamphlet on the table. It was *Tract XC*.'[24] Tait's biographers remarked that, as soon as he had read the Tract, he felt that some form of public protest was urgently needed and decided to write something himself. He drafted a letter which was never sent. The unimaginative Tait did not comprehend the subtlety of a mind such as Newman's. He wrote to A. P. Stanley on 16 April 1841 that Newman's 'Jesuitry' was derived 'not from dishonesty, but from a natural defect, a strange bent of genius that loves tortuous paths, perhaps partly because it requires an exercise of ingenuity to get along in them'.[25] The four tutors addressed a letter to Newman as 'the Editor of the *Tracts for the Times*'. They alleged that *Tract 90* might be used by persons of Roman Catholic views as justifying their position. They complained that *Tract 90* suggested that 'certain very important errors of the Church of Rome are not condemned by the Articles of the Church of England'. The letter was quite a short document and it concluded by calling 'your attention to the impropriety of such questions being treated in an anonymous publication' and expressed the 'earnest hope that you may be authorized to make known the writer's name'.[26]

Newman's identity as the author was hardly a secret, but because it was unacknowledged it added fuel to the blaze and provided the opportunity for the next attack. This was much more official, but was again initiated by Golightly who, with 'pertinacity which resembled fanaticism',[27] called upon the Vice-Chancellor (Dr Wynter). Golightly persuaded him to bring the Tracts before the Heads of Houses (Colleges). The Heads claimed that in Newman's Tract 'modes of interpretation were suggested, and have since been advocated in other publications purporting to be written by members of the University, by which subscription to the Articles might be reconciled with the adoption of Roman Catholic error'.[28] Wynter submitted the Tract to the Hebdomadal Council on 10 March 1841. Keble specifically declared that he had supported the publication of the Tract. He and Pusey each wrote to the Vice-Chancellor indicating their support for the Tract and its author, although in private they both had 'used the liberty of friendship to criticize it'. Their efforts were of no avail, the weight of their positions as holders of professorships did not assist Newman as they must have hoped. The motion of censure was passed by 19 votes to two. The action of the Board was to appoint a committee and, as Pusey put it, 'to issue a programme condemning *Tract XC*'. The following morning, on Newman's behalf, Pusey called upon Hawkins, the Provost of Oriel College, and asked him to secure a short delay 'until Newman should have published his explanations, which would be not later than the 16th'. Newman wrote to the Provost to the same effect on Sunday, 14 March. On Monday 15 March, the Board met and whatever effort Hawkins made was to no avail. There was no delay, and Newman was not given a chance to make his case. The Board's condemnation was published on the morning of Tuesday 16 March, and Newman's explanatory defence appeared later the same day. It was a pamphlet which took the form of an 'open' *Letter addressed to the Reverend Dr R. W. Jelf.*[29] Jelf was an old friend. He had been at school with Pusey and had conducted his marriage ceremony. He had also been an acquaintance of Newman's over many years, but had not been involved in any of the Tractarian controversies. He was, therefore, an ideal person for Newman to address his explanation, which ran to 30 pages. Friends who had been dismayed by *Tract 90* and the immediate turn of events, such as William Palmer of Worcester College, A.P. Perceval and W. F. Hook, the vicar of Leeds who had been an undergraduate with Pusey, now rallied to his defence.

In effect, Newman was accused of both 'Romanism' and dishonesty, and now the accusation had the sanction of the University. After his letter to Jelf, his second line of defence was to be another to the Bishop of Oxford. Systematically, Newman developed a refutation of each of the tutors' accusations. From Anglican history, he was able to cite an impressive assembly of divines in support of his claims. He turned to Bramhall, Bull, Wake, Stillingfleet, Laud and, finally, Jeremy Taylor to show that Tractarian Anglicanism did not look to Rome for its authenticity. Part of his position was to maintain 'that we have open questions'. He was not introducing any 'novelty', merely claiming a liberty that was already in the Articles, that 'our church allows a great diversity in doctrine'. The clear implication of this was that the same freedom should be allowed to High Churchmen as was claimed by Calvinists, evangelicals and liberals within the Church of England.

Newman claimed that he sought to deepen the 'religious mind of our Church' and, as a result, there was a need to address the matter of the Thirty-Nine Articles. His desire for liberty of interpretation was compounded by the circumstances of the time. He believed that there was a genuine development of interest in the Church's doctrine and life. It had been fuelled, in part, by 'great names in our literature' and he listed Sir Walter Scott, William Wordsworth and Coleridge.[30] He did not want this upsurge to benefit the Roman Catholic Church, which he repeated was in need of reform, or be allowed to dissipate itself into unorthodox or sectarian practices. Newman clearly believed that the Church of England had an opportunity and a responsibility. Consequently, there was a need to recover Anglicanism's catholic heritage if only 'to keep members of our Church from straggling in the direction of Rome'.[31] In advocating Catholicism, he was referring to the Catholicism of the patristic period which was also the true, if neglected, heritage of the Church of England. For this, Newman was not at all apologetic, although he did express his 'great sorrow that I have at all startled or offended those for whom I have nothing but respectful and kind feelings'. This, he asserted, was the position he had taken all along. However, privately he had reached a point in his thinking where he disliked criticizing Roman Catholicism. Within a few days Newman produced a second edition of the *Letter to Jelf*, with what Pusey described as 'an important postscript'.

These efforts came too late to save Newman from the obloquy of the Hebdomadal Board. The only excuse that the Board can have had for criticizing the Tract without hearing its author was that they considered it to be a less unpleasant matter to condemn an anonymous pamphlet, even when all were privately sure of the author's identity. To condemn an identified author meant that they would then have to face the prospect of pursuing that person through the University's disciplinary procedures. The Vice-Chancellor and his colleagues hoped to stop Newman's activities without engaging in open conflict. The expediency of this course of action was demonstrated a few months later when the Vice-Chancellor had to deal with a formal complaint against one of Pusey's University sermons. Further, as long as the pretence of unknown authorship could be maintained, it was not necessary to consider acting against his associates, even though they had declared their support.

The condemnation took two main forms. First, the Hebdomadal Board dissociated the University from the *Tracts for the Times*. Everyone knew that the Tracts were not in any way official publications put out by the University of Oxford. Most of them had been published in London by Rivingtons, although many people spoke of 'The Oxford Tracts'. The main condemnation, however, was that in *Tract 90* the author was 'evading rather than explaining the sense of the Thirty-Nine Articles[32], and reconciling subscription to them with the adoption of errors which they were designed to counteract'. It was this observation that impugned Newman's honesty. Newman was unhappily aware of this double standard. Reinterpretations in a liberal direction had been common almost since the Articles were promulgated. As recently as the previous year, Archbishop Whately had presented a petition in the House of Lords seeking 'to make the articles agree with the practice of the clergy'.[33] It also did not ring true when set in the context of earlier attempts made by other churchmen to get round the Thirty-Nine Articles in Oxford and elsewhere. Indeed A. P. Stanley, no friend of Tractarianism, was anxious that the activities of Tait, and his colleagues, would deny the freedom of thought claimed by men who interpreted the Articles very differently from Newman. Stanley was in Rome in March 1841, and wrote from there to Tait, 'do not draw these Articles too tight, or they will strangle more parties than one. I assure you, when I read the monition of the Heads I felt the halter at my own throat'.[34]

There was no respite in the controversy after the Heads of Houses issued their condemnation, and the next two weeks saw an extraordinary and confusing amount of activity. The Bishop of Oxford, Richard Bagot, found himself caught up in the storm and under a great deal of pressure from those opposed to the *Tracts for the Times*. He may have had some sympathy with the Tractarians' aims, but it was limited and he did not fully share their views. Nevertheless, he was a courteous man, and was not in favour of precipitate action against the authors, although he regretted the publication of *Tract 90*. Bagot saw a distinction between his role and that of the University authorities; he said the two 'stand very differently'. He said, 'my responsibility as a Bishop involves control over those who are to *give* instruction, not merely (as in the case of the University) over those who are to receive it'.[35]

However, he could not ignore *Tract 90*. The ensuing correspondence and interviews contributed to Newman's personal unsettlement. In order to avoid an outright clash with Newman, the Bishop wrote at first to Pusey on 17 March 1841, the day after the Hebdomadal Board's judgement. He enclosed a separate letter to Newman, and it seems likely that both Bagot and Newman were glad to have Pusey as an intermediary. Bagot said that his 'letter to Mr Newman is not the consequence of the judgement passed on the Tract in Oxford'.[36] He went on to express his concern that the 'grounds for alarm and offence' that might be found within *Tract 90* should be removed and that such action could be done most appropriately by the author of the Tract. He told Pusey that it would be helpful if Newman would 'disavow' such opinions, and that it would be even more so if Newman 'could adopt respectful language (and the more cordial the better) in speaking of the formularies of the Church'. This, the Bishop thought, would 'relieve the minds of many', himself included. The Bishop's letter to Pusey was a lengthy one, and that to Newman almost as long. Bagot referred to Newman's response to an Episcopal Charge which he had issued in 1838: 'under a mistaken supposition that a general censure had been contained in that Charge against . . . the *Tracts for the Times*, you offered to withdraw any tracts over which you had control, if such should be my wish'.[37] This reminder emboldened the Bishop to feel that what he had to say would be 'received in a spirit of kindness'. Bagot hoped that 'discussions upon the Articles should not be continued in the publication of the *Tracts for the Times*'. Newman said in reply that there would be no further discussion of the Articles in the *Tracts for the Times* but robbed his concession of its magnanimity by avowing, 'nor indeed was it at all my intention that there should be'.[38]

It was not unusual for Bagot to consult the Archbishop of Canterbury and he seems to have been in early contact with him. Howley wrote a letter which appeared to be an attempt to stiffen the Bishop of Oxford's resolve. Perceptively, Howley hoped that Newman's friends would

> not pledge themselves to the support of his opinions, merely because they are his, without regard to their correctness. The disposition of generous minds not to abandon a friend when he is involved in difficulties has led at various times to the establishment of permanent schisms in the Church.[39]

Howley was very uneasy about *Tract 90*, but he hoped that Bagot's actions, combined with the evident reasonableness of Newman and Pusey, might be enough to quieten the situation. This was a miscalculation, because the Tractarians' opponents had no intention of letting the matter lie. Bagot continued to be criticized for his apparent inactivity, so he increased the pressure on Newman. He invited Newman to write a letter to him containing 'a general avowal of cordial attachment to the Church of England, and disapprobation of Romish doctrines'. This was to be used as a public document, because by it Bagot would 'be exculpated from a charge of indifference and negligence of duty'.[40] Further, he hoped that the Tractarians would not carry their argument forward but would rest content with their achievements. It began to look as though Bagot and Howley wanted concessions from Newman and his friends. Certainly, this is what Newman thought.

> I am pained to see that authorities in London have increased their demands according to my submissiveness. When they thought me obstinate, they spoke only of not writing more in the Tracts about the Articles. When they find me obedient, they add the stopping of the Tracts and the suppression of No. 90. They use me against myself.[41]

It was the luckless Pusey who had the task of explaining Newman's position to the Bishop of Oxford. He acted with a shrewd appreciation of the Bishop's desire to be seen as an independent authority and not to be merely reflecting the Hebdomadal Board. Pusey pointed out that if Newman suppressed *Tract 90* at the Bishop's behest, he 'would feel that he had no right to hold a cure in your Lordship's diocese'.[42] It is unclear whether Pusey was conveying a threat by Newman, who was clearly feeling wretched about the situation. For the Bishop, the prospect of the resignation of the most troublesome priest in his diocese might be a pastoral failure, but he would have been excused from regarding it as a catastrophe. However, Pusey reported on

25 March, Newman was willing 'silently' to withdraw *Tract 90* and accept the Bishop's recommendation that the *Tracts for the Times* should cease. Pusey visited the Bishop at Cuddesdon the following day. Before he set out, however, he received three more letters from Newman! The final one was headed 'more last words'. It pointed out that there was little need to suppress all the earlier Tracts as 'editions are exhausted'. So, evidently, was Newman for he wrote, 'I much doubt whether I shall have heart to write any letter to the bishop at all.' Pusey took the three letters in his pocket, read them to Bagot and left them with him. Bagot 'read them over and over again' after he had gone. Pusey made the point that the cessation of the series of Tracts at the Bishop's unpublicized request, was, in itself, a considerable concession by Newman and his friends, but that their suppression at the public request of the Bishop was altogether a more serious act. The first option could be accepted by the Tractarians as a 'prudential precaution' by the Bishop, the second could only be seen as an act of condemnation. For the first time, Pusey introduced the likely verdict of history. He claimed that if the Bishop put a stop to the Tracts it would,

> however mildly conveyed, make a great change in the aspect they will bear in history. It is a very different thing from their having been closed naturally by their authors. It does set a sort of mark upon their close and (one need not shrink from owning) put some disgrace upon it.

Pusey could not think of a similar situation in which such widely disseminated material had been stopped 'at the recommendation of a Bishop'.[43] He raised the matter of Hampden's Bampton Lectures in his letter to Bagot. He pointed out that Hampden had been 'virtually condemned' by the University of Oxford on the grounds of his heretical teaching and for 'explaining away the doctrines of the Articles'. Despite this, however, 'no Bishop took the slightest notice of it'.[44]

Notwithstanding this reference to Hampden, it is clear that the parties were edging towards an agreement, or at least an accommodation. The following day, 27 March, Bagot wrote once more enclosing a letter from Howley which was dated 26 March 1841. It was a judicious epistle, but its date suggests that Bagot and Howley had previously agreed on their plans and that the Bishop of Oxford had successfully gained what they wanted from Newman and Pusey. The Archbishop was pleased that Bagot had avoided a censure which would, in his view, have gained 'a temporary popularity' for Bagot but at the cost of opening 'a breach, which might have been irreparable'.[45] Pusey said that he trusted 'that everything now is looking to a peaceful close, though there will be some echoes of the storm, and that a bright and calm evening will succeed a threatening morning'.[46] Newman produced a second and corrected edition of *Tract 90* on the same day and the Archbishop, who had been sent Newman's three letters to Pusey of 26 March, acknowledged Newman's points. He suggested that *Tract 90* should indeed be included in the published collection of all the Tracts. His motive was that, in this way, less attention would be drawn to the particular Tract in future and that it would not become an item to be sought by 'the curious in books'. However, he recommended that with the Tract should be included the *Letter to Dr Jelf* and other writings by Newman which were 'condemnatory of the errors of Rome'. These would combine as a way of 'explaining the real views of the writer'.[47] Howley also opined that Keble's proposed Tract on mysticism, which was to be a continuation of *Tract 89*, should go ahead but not as *Tract 91*, but rather as 'second part' of the original. Pusey knew that Keble had no objection to the non-appearance of the second part of his Tract on mysticism, because the whole work could easily be brought together in the form of a book. A proposed Tract by Pusey on the Apocrypha should be abandoned, or (if not) published in a different format so as to disassociate it from the *Tracts for the Times*.

Newman agreed to produce a public *Letter to the Right Reverend Richard, Lord Bishop of Oxford*, and set to work at once. It was published on 31 March 1841 and began with the customary studied politeness that characterized such publications. Newman remarked on the unusual fact that a clergyman should write publicly to his bishop 'instead of silently obeying' the message which he had received.[48] As with his *Letter to Dr Jelf*, much of the substance of this document was in the form of quotations from earlier writings. This is part of the explanation of how Newman was able to compile it so quickly. He believed that the use of quotations from earlier work was a demonstration of his consistency. More importantly, it also confirmed his loyalty to the Church of England, for he was merely repeating words he had written in less controversial times, when no questions hung over his loyalty and integrity. In order to strengthen this assertion Newman also alluded to his conservative management of services in St Mary's during his incumbency.[49] This is an observation which is interesting in its own right as he was writing well before the development of ritualism came to be associated with the Oxford Movement and the Tractarians. As he drew to a conclusion, Newman admitted that he had 'seriously contemplated, some time since, the resignation of [his] Living'. He had been kept from doing so 'by the advice of a friend to whom I feel I ought to submit myself',[50] but the situation had been brought back to his mind by the condemnation of *Tract 90* by the Heads of Houses, to which he referred only 'for the purpose of assuring your Lordship of the great sorrow it gives me to have incurred their disapprobation'.[51] The mention of resignation, however, was not something he was again contemplating.

Towards the end of the *Letter* Newman used the existence of the correspondence that lay behind it as further evidence of his loyalty to the Church of England. This protestation may have had a deeper meaning than its apparently conventional sentiments. He was acutely aware of Bagot's correspondence with Archbishop Howley and may have believed, or wished to believe, that this *Letter*, written at the invitation of the former and with the concurrence of the latter, would remove the prospect of wider episcopal condemnation from himself and from what he had said in *Tract 90*. It was to prove a forlorn hope. Or he may have been preparing his grounds, consciously or not, for justifying more drastic action at some future date.

The optimism engendered by the conclusion of this complicated series of exchanges was to be short-lived. *Tract 90* had attracted a great deal of publicity that had agitated bishops other than Bagot and Archbishop Howley. It was unfortunate that at this time a significant proportion of the bishops were preparing formal addresses, or 'Charges', to their clergy. Such Charges were usually in the form of advice and admonition, but doctrinal and disciplinary matters were also referred to. No doubt, most were unaware of the exchanges with Newman, but they were aware of the agitation which the Tract had caused among the clergy and laity at large. A significant number of them felt that the Tract needed to be noticed and commented upon in Charges which they were preparing, although Bagot had told Newman that only 'two or three' were likely to mention it. Without exception those comments were hostile. It was possible that some hostility could have been avoided if Pusey had taken the advice of Benjamin Harrison. Howley had discussed the matter with Harrison who suggested to Pusey that he 'should write a letter to the Archbishop, with a view to placing before the Episcopal Bench the grounds on which a more favourable judgement of the Oxford Tracts might be formed'.[52] Harrison thought this idea to be good, and also timely. Pusey, however, characteristically hesitated because the request did not come expressly from the Archbishop. In due course he did write, but by then it was too late. Episcopal Charges began to be issued. Without the benefit of an explanatory gloss giving the Tractarians' considered views, a significant number of bishops condemned *Tract 90*. Newman was at once in an impossible position. The Tractarian Movement was 'undoubtedly, among other things, a reassertion of Episcopal authority'.[53] Consequently, Newman was in the awkward position of being condemned by the very authority which he had idealized and sought to enhance. The dilemma was not resolvable. Towards the end of 1841 and in 1842, the Episcopal Charges continued to appear. Many bishops took the opportunity to condemn the teachings of the Tractarians. Even Bagot himself added words of criticism. It was the combined weight of such criticism that nearly broke Newman's spirit. Indeed, it was the second of three 'blows' which, in his *Apologia*, he recognized as fatal to his continuing position within the Church of England.

Nearly 40 years after these events, Pusey reminisced: 'I remember Newman saying to me at Littlemore, "Oh, Pusey! we have leant upon the Bishops, and they have broken down under us!" It was too late to say anything; he was already leaving us!'[54] Pusey went on to observe that he had not personally 'leant upon the Bishops', but rather upon the Church, but it was true of Newman. Consequently, the condemnations within the Charges were enormously significant, particularly when it is recalled that Newman probably had derived an unjustifiable sense of security from the knowledge that the Archbishop was associated with Bagot's efforts.

Pusey was aware of what his friend was going through and was at last moved to follow Harrison's suggestion that he should write to Archbishop Howley. He expressed himself forcibly: 'The Bishops' Charges have been made the occasion of attacks, too often, alas! from the pulpit, and that in language little fitted for the sanctuary of God . . .'. Perversely, as he observed, individuals who wished to destroy the Church 'still plead the authority of our Bishops'. In addition to these outrages, 'thoughtful sermons' had been 'blasphemously commented upon and ridiculed'. This was undoubtedly a reference to the harsh treatment which he had received in the summer of 1841 for his University Sermon. Pusey was also severely critical of 'blasphemous writing in the worst part' of the press, 'the influence of which was greater than its commitment to accuracy of reporting'. He went on to declare that the failure of the bishops was likely to be a contributory factor in deterring men from ordination at a time when God seemed to be calling an increasing number of able individuals 'into Holy Orders'.

He predicted that the condemnatory stance of so many bishops would add to the attractiveness of the Roman Catholic Church for 'the young [who] are guided by their sympathies rather than their convictions'.[55] Pusey was very conscious of the irony of what he predicted.

Outside Oxford, it was unfortunate that the House of Commons was debating the matter of increasing the financial support for the Roman Catholic seminary at Maynooth College in the week after the publication of *Tract 90*. Maynooth had been founded in 1795 and, by an extraordinary anomaly, was supported by an annual grant from Parliament. Lord Morpeth, defending the grant and the proposed increase, pointed out that Parliament had been fully aware of the religious allegiance of Maynooth when making the grant. He then asserted that this demonstrated a consistency which was lacking in a certain 'Protestant University'. With this gratuitous insult the unfortunate Newman received another blow. Newman was grievously hurt by the controversy over *Tract 90*. He began to withdraw from Oxford life, conscious that his position was intolerable. Gradually he perceived that he should become a Roman Catholic. He did not move, however, until he was sure in his own mind that the decision was a positive one, and not a reaction to the way in which he had been treated. The consequences of the treatment which he received over *Tract 90* were momentous for him, and grave for the Oxford Movement.

Chapter 5

Contending with Setbacks

For the Tractarians 1841 got off to a hesitant start, but it was to be an eventful time. Early in the year they launched a new project, similar in concept to the *Library of the Fathers*. It was the *Library of Anglo-Catholic Theology*.[1] It was an endeavour to make available the post-Reformation Anglican texts which supported the Tractarian theological position. A precursor had been Keble's work on Richard Hooker's *Laws of Ecclesiastical Polity*. In the context of the new series, the use of the term 'Anglo-Catholic' was strictly correct. It had originally been coined in the seventeenth century, and was not taken over by the followers of the Tractarians to describe themselves until the last quarter of the nineteenth century. Surprisingly, for another demonstration of the Oxford Movement's commitment to sound learning, the scheme did not attract the same degree of commitment from the leaders as had the *Library of the Fathers*. Nevertheless, it was important and ran for over 20 years and eventually produced 88 volumes.

Keble worked on it, but complained when a scholar preferred it to continuing with other work for the *Library of the Fathers*. Pusey also worked on the plan, but with no great enthusiasm, and until the events of 1845 removed him from the scene, Newman was also involved. He too was never really enthused by the project, but probably because it began at the time when he was becoming disillusioned with the Church of England. William Palmer of Worcester College and W. J. Copeland also worked on the scheme, but others from the next generation made the major contributions. In addition to Bishop Wilson, writers who were republished in the *Library of*

Anglo-Catholic Theology included Bishop Cosin of Durham, Archbishop Bramhall of Armagh and Archbishop William Laud.[2]

The summer of 1841 saw the development of a crisis which was outside the control or influence of the Tractarians. It was the first of several in what was to be a difficult year, but their reaction was muted because they were not entirely of one mind at the start. The problem was a proposal for a bishopric to be set up in Jerusalem. The idea had a political origin which predated the controversy. The French and the Russians each held protectorates in the Middle East which were meant to look after the interests of the Roman and Greek Christians. Britain and Prussia were keen to restrict their influence. Combined with this ill-defined objective was a religious ambition of King Frederick William IV of Prussia. He wanted to overcome what he saw to be a deficiency within his country's Church, which was a comparatively recent combination of Lutheranism and Calvinism. He believed that it ought to incorporate episcopacy into its government, but there was opposition to the idea within Prussia, although Dean Church was to claim 'no German cared a straw about it'.[3] Someone, probably the Chevalier C. C. J. Bunsen, had the idea to establish a 'Protestant Bishopric' in Jerusalem which would be supported by the British and the Prussian governments. In this way it was felt that episcopacy could be quietly introduced in the Prussian Church and that the necessary corrective would be introduced into middle eastern politics.

The proposal was that the Church of England would supply the episcopal ordination of the man selected, that the two Churches would nominate candidates for appointment in turn and that the costs would be shared by the two countries. The new bishopric would care for the Anglicans and the German Protestants who happened to live in Palestine. Bunsen came to England to discuss the proposal, and was met with some enthusiasm. The English ecclesiastics with whom he negotiated were Archbishop Howley and Bishop Blomfield of London. With their general support for the scheme, the government went ahead with the necessary legislation. There was also support from some evangelicals, notably Anthony Ashley Cooper who later became Lord Shaftesbury and was related to Pusey. His primary enthusiasm was that the appointment could help restore the Jews to Palestine and lead to their conversion to Christianity in order to bring about the second coming of Christ. It was also welcomed by liberal theologians such as Arnold as being a move towards a comprehensive Protestant Church. With Convocation inactive, the scheme could not be considered by the Church at large. The Archbishop himself introduced the Foreign Bishoprics Bill in the House of Lords on 30 August 1841, and events moved rapidly. The Royal Assent was given on 5 October. Michael Solomon Alexander, a convert from orthodox Judaism, was chosen to be the first bishop. Shaftesbury was pleased at the selection of Alexander, believing that the appointment was, as a later writer described it, a 'slap in the face for the Tractarians'.[4]

Newman and Keble were utterly opposed to the idea. In their minds, the Prussian Church was heretical, and Newman said so. Consequently, it was entirely out of order to give the blessing of episcopacy to such a body. Not all High Churchmen agreed. Indeed, Pusey did not at first register any sort of protest, which Liddon attributed to the warm friendship which existed between Bunsen and Pusey's brother. It may also have been due to the fact that he had studied in Germany as a young man, although he already regretted his early enthusiasm for German theology. He did, however, hope that the Prussian Protestants 'would be absorbed into our Church . . . and be Catholicised', and he was under the impression that there was a community in Jerusalem which the bishop would superintend.[5] W. F. Hook even published a pamphlet to help with fund-raising, and Benjamin Harrison and William Palmer of Worcester College were far from hostile. Among the laymen who supported the scheme was W. E. Gladstone, who was initially a trustee. Later he published a strongly expressed critique of the plan. Newman also wrote a strong protest which he sent to the Bishop of Oxford on 13 November, but Bagot pleaded that as he had not been consulted he was unable to do anything. The rest of the bishops were in a similar position.

Pusey had spent a large part of the summer vacation in Ireland. This was for the benefit of his children and also provided him with an opportunity to visit some Irish sisterhoods. When he returned, he visited the Archbishop at Addington Palace and had a lengthy discussion with him and Harrison. This caused him to doubt the qualities of the chosen candidate for the bishopric, but not to oppose the concept. He was more dismayed when he discovered that the congregation at Jerusalem amounted only to four persons! These factors helped Pusey to change his mind. He admitted to Newman that he could do nothing publicly having given Bunsen his initial support. However, he also told Newman that he had written to Jelf, 'embodying all your strongest language as my own'. Jelf had forwarded the letter to the Bishop of London and Pusey grimly joked 'probably such language has not found its way to him before'. Pusey was also aware that the matter was unsettling for others, such as Frederick Oakeley, with whom he was in correspondence, and W. G. Ward who were at the 'Romanizing' end of the Tractarian group. He was uneasy as to the ultimate reaction of such men.

Michael Alexander was consecrated bishop in the chapel of Lambeth Palace on 7 November. He set out for Jerusalem and arrived on 22 January 1842. Immediately after the consecration, William Palmer, of Magdalen College, and Newman wrote independently to the Archbishop of Canterbury. Newman's latter was the more weighty, and Keble and Pusey both read and approved of it although Keble, characteristically, asked for 'a little expression of reverence to those whom you are censuring'. Howley took no notice of either communication because it was simply too late. With the consecration of Alexander, there was nothing to be done, and the issue fell away until a successor was needed some years later when wider consultation was undertaken. In fact the appointment eventually became an entirely Anglican affair. However, by that time the damage was done. Newman was to claim later that the matter of the Jerusalem bishopric was instrumental among the factors that eventually caused him to convert to Roman Catholicism: 'it brought me on to the beginning of the end'.[6]

The next controversy in which the Tractarians were embroiled reveals the contempt in which their theological views were held by a significant number of senior members of Oxford University. It also reveals a disregard for natural justice. A sermon by Pusey was the cause of the storm. It was preached in St Mary's church in May 1841, the fourth Sunday after Easter, two months after the censure of Newman's *Tract 90*. It was a formal sermon preached 'before the University'. Such sermons were, in effect, demonstrations of the intimate link that bound Oxford University to the Church of England. Until Parliament reformed the University Statutes, Oxford was virtually a Church of England institution. Every member had to subscribe to the Thirty-Nine Articles of Religion and to be a communicant member of the Church. Such was the situation when Pusey ascended the pulpit of St Mary's church.

Pusey's line of thought is well summarized by the title which he eventually gave the sermon, 'The Holy Eucharist, a Comfort to the Penitent'. He planned it as one of a series which would show how God has provided for those consciences which were worried about post-baptismal sin. Pusey was seeking to answer, in a practical way, the distress which his series of Tracts on baptism had caused some scrupulous people. In the sermon Pusey drew heavily on the Early Fathers, and specifically did not adopt the Roman Catholic doctrine of transubstantiation as an explanation of the presence of Christ in the Eucharist. J. B. Mozley heard the sermon and remarked on it as

> useful . . . eloquent . . . striking . . . beautiful . . . it was a long sermon . . . not longer than usual. It was, of course, said to contain high doctrinal views . . . but as all Dr Pusey's sermons contain high views, there was nothing to draw attention in this remark . . . .[7]

Afterwards the Vice-Chancellor, Dr Wynter, and the Provost of Oriel College, Hawkins, left the church together and agreed, as they walked, that they did not much like what they had heard. Wynter, a kind-hearted man who was not strong enough to handle conflict successfully, later recorded that they felt it unadvisable to take any sort of action against the preacher. However, on the Tuesday the Vice-Chancellor received a formal complaint that he was obliged to follow up. The University Statutes had a procedure for assessing the orthodoxy of any sermon against which a complaint was lodged and, if proven, condemn and punish the preacher. The arrangement was that six Doctors of Divinity would investigate the allegation and adjudicate. Under the arrangements which had been made to accommodate the Hampden situation, the Lady Margaret Professor was one of the judges. It was at this point that Pusey began to be the victim of injustice, because the complainant was a man named Faussett and he was the Lady Margaret Professor of Divinity! As he was obliged to do, Wynter asked Pusey for a copy of the sermon, but did not reveal the name of the person who had complained. Pusey obliged on 22 May, having asked for a few days in which to annotate the sermon and signify the specifically patristic passages. This was, as he wrote to Newman, with a touch of grim ironic humour, 'that they might not be exposed unconsciously to condemn e.g. St Cyril of Alexandria when they thought they were only condemning me'.[8] He asked for a hearing before the panel of assessors and sent the sermon to Wynter with a characteristically long letter.

The Vice-Chancellor had, in the meantime, set about appointing six doctors as judges. In addition to Faussett, they were Dr Jenkyns, the Master of Balliol; Dr Symons, the Warden of Wadham, and Dr Ogilvie, the Regius Professor of Pastoral Theology. The fifth man was Pusey's old friend Dr Jelf, who felt it necessary to explain to Pusey that he accepted the obligation in the hope of reducing the harm that might be done. The sixth judge was none other than Provost Hawkins of Oriel, and a man who long had a difficult relationship with the

Tractarians and with whom Wynter had already discussed the sermon. They met for the first time on 24 May with Wynter as their chairman and arranged to meet again on 27 May. They agreed that each would bring a written judgement on the sermon to the second meeting. Pusey was not permitted to attend either meeting even though he had asked to be present, which he believed the University Statutes permitted. He was refused on the grounds that, although the Statutes did not deny the accused the right to attend, they did not require attendance. Not only was he denied the opportunity to explain himself and to defend what he had said, he did not even know the specific charges against him and did not learn the identity of his accuser through any official channels. Naturally, Pusey and his supporters felt this to be an injustice and Liddon, in his very full account in the biography of Pusey, made a good deal of it. At the end of the second meeting Wynter declared that Pusey was guilty of the charge made against him, 'namely, that he had preached certain things which were either dissonant from or contrary to the doctrine of the Church of England'.[9] Jelf refused to join in the condemnation of the sermon.

Having found their man guilty, the Vice-Chancellor had to decide whether to seek a recantation on Pusey's part, or whether to suspend him for a time from preaching University sermons. There was some disagreement among the judges over the form of sentence. It would have been appropriate for the Vice-Chancellor to send for Pusey and ask whether he would recant. Wynter did not do this, perhaps fearing the reply he would get. The unfortunate Jelf found himself in the impossible position of having to act on Wynter's behalf, and he was sent to see Pusey. As might be expected, Pusey was not willing to recant but he had a serious conversation with Jelf. Unwisely he did agree that he would keep secret all the communications between himself, the judges and the Vice-Chancellor. This concession damaged even more his chances of receiving just treatment. It allowed Wynter and the other judges to proceed with the sentence of suspension without any hindrance. A considerable amount of negotiations followed, and were chronicled by Liddon, who had the advantage of the Vice-Chancellor's private notes which were made available to him many years later. Following Pusey's discussion with Jelf, the judges met for a third time, and Wynter sent Jelf to Pusey on 2 June 1841 to inform him of the sentence, a suspension for two years.

Pusey immediately decided to issue a protest. His grounds were that the basis of his guilt had not been expressed, and that he had been denied an opportunity to justify or explain his views to the judges. The publication of Pusey's protest was the first public indication that anything had happened since the sermon had been sent for. As events unrolled, the judges found themselves in a dilemma. They had refused to give Pusey a hearing, but now did not wish to be seen to have condemned him unheard. As a result, half-truths and misinformation began to get out. Pusey protested further that as he had kept rigorously to the secrecy requirements and had not even told his closest friends of what was happening, so he expected silence from the other side. 'Unless equal silence is imposed upon all', he said, 'I must regard the understanding at an end, and myself released from an engagement which was understood to be mutual'.[10] An Address was sent to the Vice-Chancellor, signed by 61 resident members of the University, asking for the publication of the grounds for the sentence. Wynter reacted angrily. A second Address was sent, signed by 230 non-resident members of the Convocation. This also elicited a bad-tempered reply from Wynter. He impertinently reminded the signatories of their obligations under the oaths taken when they had received their degrees. It did not escape notice that among those reprimanded in this way were W. E. Gladstone and Mr Justice Coleridge, both of whom had signed the second Address. Another, seemingly disingenuous, enquiry reached the Vice-Chancellor from a clergyman who was anxious on behalf of all who were to preach University sermons and who might, unwittingly, bring disciplinary action upon themselves.

As the process wore on and it became apparent that Pusey would stand condemned and not get any sort of hearing, it was inevitable that he should think of publishing the sermon. It was entirely in keeping with his character that he should agonize over the matter of publication. Reluctantly he decided to go ahead, having sought advice from Keble, Newman, Gladstone and perhaps others. An introduction was written by Pusey and amended by Newman. He accepted Keble's reservation that he should not dedicate the publication to Newman as a way of demonstrating his loyalty to his friend following the *Tract 90* debacle. Keble was also in favour of the production of a *catena* of Anglican authorities, to be compiled by Newman's curate W. J. Copeland, as an appendix to the published sermon. These suggestions were accepted by Pusey and the sermon appeared with them at the end of June. Also published with it was 'a large apparatus of notes, mainly patristic, intended to show that the doctrinal language of the sermon was throughout, either in the letter or in substance, that of the primitive fathers of the Church'.[11] With the contents of the sermon permanently in the public domain, people were able to judge its ortho-doxy for themselves, and Pusey began to receive support from outside his immediate circle.

Pusey decided that there might be ground for redress through the Court of Arches, the principal ecclesiastical court, and accordingly took advice. He planned to trigger an action by inviting a personal friend named Woodgate to delate his sermon to Bishop Bagot. Almost inevitably, Bagot consulted the Archbishop of Canterbury. He coun-selled against the idea on the ground that for a friend to seek the action in the expectation of vindicating the preacher was not a straightforward use of the court's process. Bagot agreed, and also pointed out, rather feebly, that an ecclesiastical court would have to establish who exactly had preached an offending sermon before taking action. In the face of these rebuffs, Pusey was forced to abandon his plans for legal redress. Much the same applied when he considered taking action more locally in the University, by invoking the intervention of the Vice-Chancellor's Court. In the end, he had no redress and had to endure the sentence of suspension from preaching 'before the University' for two years. He sought the comfort of knowing that he was not condemned by Bishop Bagot, whom he believed to hold a good opinion of him. He therefore asked Bagot to declare publicly that he did not condemn the doctrine of the sermon. The cautious Bagot did not do so, and so Pusey was denied even that small consolation. Pusey piled a further inhibition on himself, by deciding that he would not preach anywhere without the express permission of his diocesan bishop.

'There was', Liddon observed, 'no more to be done: Pusey had to wait for more than a year until his next University sermon gave the opportunity of repeating, without challenge, all the doctrine for which he had been condemned'.[12] When the inhibition expired, he returned at once to the battle. His next University Sermon was preached in 1846. It was published with the title, *The Entire Absolution of the Penitent*. In the mean time, he had the support of many friends and of the increasing number of unknown clergy and others who were being won over to the views of the Tractarians in Oxford and elsewhere. Liddon did not fail to note with irony an inconsistency which occurred shortly afterwards. The University of Oxford at that time was part of the nation's Christian establishment. Indeed a recent writer has described it as 'little more than the Church of England at its books'.[13] The American ambassador, a Mr Everett, who was a Socinian (or Unitarian), was given an honorary degree of DCL in 1843. The inconsistency was that Everett was accorded a high honour, although he denied the divinity of Christ, by a University which had recently condemned the sacramental language of one of its own professors. The event did not pass without protest, and the degree was conferred amid uproar.

The opponents of the Tractarians who had worked to silence Pusey within the University soon had another opportunity to register their disapproval of the Tractarians. John Keble reached the end of his second and final period of office as Professor of Poetry at the end of 1841, before the furore over the Jerusalem bishopric and Pusey's sermon had died away. There was a general level of expectation among the Tractarians and their friends that he would be succeeded by one of their number, Isaac Williams. He was a poet of some distinction, but was one of the few who had not taken to Keble's *Christian Year*; he 'did not much enter into it'. Some of Williams' hymns have survived for more than a century after his death. He did, however, have a real degree of notoriety after the disturbance generated by his Tracts on 'Reserve in Communicating Religious Knowledge', so his candidature was certain to be controversial. Williams' own account of the debacle over the professorship has survived in his autobiography.[14] It is written in cool tones that underplay the level of excitement which the election generated and the pain that he must have felt at the outcome. However, he could not help recording anecdotes that reveal his sense of being betrayed by one or two old friends. Among those who wrote expressing their inability to support Williams was Benjamin Harrison. Although Williams understood that Harrison was in a delicate position as the Archbishop's chaplain, he objected to the manner in which he expressed himself. Williams recorded that Harrison was estranged from his Tractarian friends for a time as a result of the election. Williams alleged that he did not seek the honour of being a candidate but was pleased with the support of his friends. He would have liked to avoid any public office, but he felt compelled to let his candidature stand. This was particularly so when he was asked to step aside in favour of another candidate from the same College (Trinity). He reached that decision when the request was combined with a statement that he would be opposed because of *Tract 80* and because of 'my church principles'. A further disadvantage for Williams was the recent publication of the notorious *Tract 90*.

Shortly afterwards the Reverend James Garbett of Brasenose College was also nominated. The Principal of Brasenose, A. S. Gilbert, who later became Bishop of Chichester, was an opponent of the Tractarians and may not have been entirely motivated by the relative suitability of the new candidate. Williams believed that Gilbert nominated Garbett 'with the prospect that a religious commotion might be excited'.[15] Garbett, for his part, was a knowledgeable man whom Liddon described as 'a critic of poetry' in relation to Williams as a poet in his own right. Garbett's supporters wrote requesting the electors' support and alluded to Williams' involvement with the Tractarians. His success in the election, it was claimed, 'would undoubtedly be represented as a decision of Convocation in favour of his party'.[16] Unfortunately this precipitated Pusey into circulating members of the University Convocation with a printed letter of his own. Although he dropped some of his fiercer remarks at Newman's suggestion, he was rather blunt and his activity sharpened the party element in the election. From the moment of the publication of Pusey's circular, the election became almost entirely a theological contest. Williams later recorded as his own view that Pusey's circular contributed to Garbett's eventual success. The next tactic by those who valued peace in the University was an attempt to persuade both candidates to withdraw. This initiative came from Gladstone through the intervention of Bishop Bagot of Oxford. Williams laid the matter before the Principal of Trinity College who pointed out that the Bishop was exceeding his jurisdiction, and so the move failed.

After Pusey's unwise intervention a rumour developed that, if Williams should lose the election by a large margin, then the University authorities might move against the Tractarians. Consequently it became necessary to discover what would be the likely outcome of the election. A comparison of pledged votes was taken, and Garbett was calculated to receive almost 300 more votes than Williams. It was prudent for Williams to withdraw, and Williams was a prudent man, but everyone regarded the outcome as another defeat for the Tractarians within their own University. No action was taken against the Tractarians, but the events gave them another, quite different, victory. The Hebdomadal Board sought to use the turn of events to remove the restrictions imposed upon Professor Hampden in 1836. This measure was put to the vote in June 1842 and failed by a similar proportion, although smaller numbers, as had proposed to vote against Williams. There was a clear sense that if the censure of Hampden had been appropriate in 1836, the situation was not sufficiently different in 1842 to merit a reversal of that decision.

Although it was noticeable that support for the Tractarians was gradually growing in the country, another reverse was not far away.

This time the eye of the storm was to be John Keble and his parish or, more accurately, his curate. One of the bishops who had issued a Charge hostile to *Tract 90* was C. R. Sumner of Winchester, an evangelical who was completely hostile to Tractarians. The new controversy had a personal element. Keble described it as 'a deliberate beginning of serious vexation on the part of authority'. His curate, a man named Peter Young, was married to Caroline Coxwell who was a cousin of Keble's wife. The relationship between the Kebles and the Youngs was excellent and Mrs Young and their eight children were frequently at Hursley Vicarage. Young was a diligent, unassuming man whose work was much appreciated by Keble. He was in deacon's orders, and in July 1841 approached the Bishop to arrange to be a candidate for ordination to the priesthood. He presented himself for the examination which was usually a formality. Keble wrote,

> he was immediately set to answer a long string of questions all tending one way: the first being, in substance, How do you govern yourself in the construction of the Thirty-nine Articles? And the last, Explain Consubstantiation, Transubstantiation, and the doctrine of our Church as differing from both.[17]

Young was competent to answer, and did so by referring to and quoting from the catechism in the Book of Common Prayer and from the Articles. He also referred to various definitive Anglican divines such as Richard Hooker. The Bishop, supported by two chaplains, demanded that he answer in his own words. After two sessions on different days, Young was sent away without being ordained and was told to 'get clearer views on the subject'. Keble felt the injustice of the situation as much as did Young who had certainly faced questions that were not asked of the other candidates. Keble wrote to Sumner. He asked if he could assist in clearing up the matter, perhaps by calling on the Bishop, fearing that there had 'been some misunderstanding'. The Bishop declined to see Keble, and recommended some reading for Young.

Pusey was about to go to Ireland for two months, as has already been noticed. Whilst there, he saw Young who was also out of England. On his return, Pusey went so far as to raise the matter with Archbishop Howley when he called on him at Addington. It is of interest that he did so when his interview with the Archbishop was at the height of the controversy over the Jerusalem bishopric. Howley took the matter seriously and subsequently wrote to Pusey but, predictably, said that he could not interfere with the way in which the Bishop of Winchester managed the clergy of his diocese. Keble felt that the Bishop was really aiming at him, and that view is certainly borne out by the tone and content of Howley's letter to Pusey on the matter. Keble decided that he would resign if Sumner called upon him to do so, which he did not. Sumner arranged to see Young on 23 July, but the outcome was unsatisfactory as he again declined to confer priest's orders on him.

Keble wondered if the matter could be resolved through the courts by the expedient of Bishop Sumner prosecuting him, not Young, for heresy. When the Bishop showed an understandable reluctance to do so, Keble hoped to provoke some theological opponent to do it. His friends persuaded him to abandon the idea, so he had to content himself with writing formal and public letters to Sumner and Howley. The stalemate persisted for many years. Young remained as Keble's curate until 1857, still only in deacon's orders. The impasse eventually ended when he was offered a living in Devon, and Bishop Phillpotts of Exeter ordained him to the priesthood.

In the series of setbacks which the Tractarians suffered at this tumultuous time, the next was both serious and protracted. William George Ward was one of the principal figures of the Romanizing group among the followers of the Tractarians, along with Frederick Oakeley. Both were Fellows of Balliol College. The Romanizing tendency in the Oxford Movement became a significant element at about the time Newman withdrew from Oxford life and began to live at Littlemore. It was Ward, however, who caused a very significant setback for the Tractarians. Born in 1812, he was elected to his Fellowship in 1834, just as the *Tracts for the Times* were becoming noticed. He had initially been attracted to the theologically liberal views of Arnold, but had changed his allegiance to Newman. He was a devout man with a strong intellect which craved logical argument, and he also had about him an air of melancholy. As a conversationalist, by contrast, he was an exciting man. Friends and foes were swept along in discussion and argument, and some found the experience exhausting. After a lengthy discussion with him, Arnold took to his bed for a day's rest. Many who engaged with him in debate felt that he pushed them further than they wished to go. He was able to disagree strongly with the views of colleagues, without feeling that such matters should damage or interfere with his friendships. By contrast, at this stage of his career, he did not express himself clearly on paper. However, he was a frequent contributor to the *British Critic* which was the organ of the Romanist section of the Oxford Movement. Newman had edited it from 1838 until April 1841 when Tom Mozley took over. Mozley's friends thought that he would convert to Roman Catholicism but he never did. His editorship was not a success and the journal closed in 1843. Mozley found Ward to be a difficult contributor and received complaints about his contributions which Dean Church described as 'vigorous and unintermittent exposition . . . without hesitation'. Ward's first full-length book was published in 1844 partly in response to the criticism generated by his *British Critic* articles and voiced by William Palmer in his *Narrative of Events*.

Ward's book had the title, *The Ideal of a Christian Church Considered in Comparison with Existing Practice*, and has correctly been described as clumsily written, ill-digested but nevertheless powerful. If Newman had been inclined to push his case too hard in *Tract 90*, Ward carried the process a good deal further in his book. He had accepted Newman's thinking about the catholic nature of the Church, but interpreted that doctrine in terms of Roman Catholicism. The basis of his book started with a view of the 'ideal' of what the Church ought to be. He then asserted that the Roman Catholic Church was the only body to fulfil completely that ideal. The Church of England, of which Ward was an ordained priest, failed to approximate with his concept of the ideal. Even this assertion did not constitute the book's real cause of offence. That came when Ward claimed to hold the full *corpus* of Roman Catholic doctrine whilst continuing to serve as an Anglican clergyman and as a Fellow of a College in what was then an entirely Anglican institution. Perhaps the most offensive passage, and certainly the most quoted, was where he wrote, 'We find, oh, most joyful, most wonderful, most unexpected sight! we find the whole cycle of Roman doctrine gradually possessing numbers of English Churchmen.' This was certainly not what Pusey and Keble, and even the troubled Newman thought at the time. Ward made his unfortunate claims even more likely to attract condemnation when he continued, 'Three years have passed since I said plainly that in subscribing the Articles I renounce no Roman doctrine; yet I retain my fellowship which I hold on tenure of subscription, and have received no ecclesiastical censure in any shape'.[18]

The book was published during the Long Vacation, so its readers had liberty to reflect upon its contents and to begin to think about a response. One thing was clear, that officialdom would have to respond. Before anything could be done, however, a fresh wave of hostility was generated against the Tractarians and must be noticed before following Ward's story. The Vice-Chancellor, Dr Wynter, had come to the end of his term of office. His handling of recent explosive events was considered by many to be inept. Wynter had been in an unassailable position, but many felt that an opportunity to protest was presented when a new man had to be appointed. Long-established custom meant that succeeding Vice-Chancellors were appointed following the simple process of seniority. This meant that the man expected to fill the post was Dr Symons, the Warden of Wadham who was noted for his hostility to the Tractarians and who had been one of the six doctors who condemned Pusey's sermon. His appointment was challenged in the University Convocation. The challenge was not originated by the Tractarians, but some of their supporters were very active in it. Keble and Pusey both had reservations, but Newman did not express an opinion. In a sense their reluctance to oppose the scheme made them partly blameworthy, for they were wrong to let the enthusiasts for the plan go ahead. When the vote was taken, Dr Symons was elected by 883 votes to 183. The opposition was completely routed and the outcome was counted as a defeat for the Tractarians. In the heated atmosphere of Oxford at the time, the move against the new Vice-Chancellor meant that action against Ward was inevitable.

A committee examined the book and, unsurprisingly, found that there was a case to answer. It was decided to bring it before the University Convocation in the Sheldonian Theatre. At a meeting set for 13 February 1845, three resolutions were to be put: (1) to condemn Ward's book; (2) to degrade him by depriving him of all his University degrees; (3) to add to the subscription to the Thirty-Nine Articles demanded by Statute the requirement that such subscription should be in the sense in which 'they were both first published and were now imposed by the University'. The first proposition was straight-forward, and Ward could have expected something like it. The second was mean-spirited and vindictive because members of the University who had become Roman Catholics had not been deprived in this way, and Ward (at the time) was still an Anglican. The third proposition was altogether of a different hue. It threatened the Tractarian Romanists, but it threatened many others as well. The 'noose' could by this measure, as Stanley feared, be tightened around the liberals' necks also. Gradually it dawned upon the authorities that the third proposition was likely to be unworkable. On 23 January it was withdrawn. Astonishingly, and an indication of how high feelings were running within the University, it was substituted shortly afterwards with a resolution condemning *Tract 90*. It is clear that there was a plan to hunt Ward in such a way as to flush out Newman who was living silently at Littlemore. Newman was not particularly worried. Indeed, he told Pusey that he would regard censure of *Tract 90* as providing the required 'external circumstances to [help] determine my cause'.[19]

The University Proctors, H. P. Guillemard of Trinity College and Richard William Church of Oriel, later Dean of St Paul's and the most important early historian of the Oxford Movement, had the power to veto resolutions placed before Convocation. On 10 February the Proctors declared that they would exercise that right with regard to the third resolution believing it was, as Liddon put it, 'inexpedient for the University'. Newman, out at Littlemore, gave no indication that he would attend and, indeed, he did not.

At the hearing on 13 February, Ward was permitted to speak in English rather than Latin, and he did so for an hour with vigour. Oakeley demonstrated his support by standing nearby. Apart from the reading of the judgement of the Hebdomadal committee, there were no speeches except Ward's. When he finished, the vote was taken. The book was condemned by 777 votes to 386, and a little later the unfortunate Ward was deprived of his degrees by 569 votes to 511. The reduction in size of the majority meant that the deprivation was a pyrrhic victory for the University authorities. The veto by the Proctors followed when the motion against *Tract 90* was put, and the proceedings ended in uproar. Later the Proctors received a letter of thanks for their action. It was signed by two hundred members of the University. Undergraduates had been kept outside the Sheldonian theatre, but they escorted Ward, who had stumbled in the snow as he left the building, back to Balliol College. Ward had recently become engaged to be married, but this was not announced until after the vote and his friends were astonished at the news. Ward and his wife converted to Roman Catholicism in September, a few weeks before Newman. Oakeley followed them shortly afterwards.

The condemnation of Ward was a catastrophe, and Dean Church used that word as the title of the last chapter of his book. In it he said that

> to ordinary lookers-on it naturally seemed that a shattering blow had been struck at the Tractarian party and their cause; struck, indeed, formally and officially . . . It was more than a defeat, it was a rout, in which they were driven and chased headlong from the field; it was a

wreck in which their boasts and hopes of the last few years met the fate which wise men had always anticipated, Oxford repudiated them.[20]

This was an overstatement, but graphically reveals how the actions of the University authorities rankled in Church's mind for many years. Newman remained silent in his Littlemore retreat.

Littlemore was a village three miles from Oxford but part of Newman's parish. For some reason he was attracted to the place and it became a sort of spiritual home, although there was no church or parsonage there. In order to carry out his pastoral duties in the village, which he took very seriously, Newman rented lodgings and also a meeting place. He employed a curate to carry out the majority of the duties, but spent a great deal of time in the village and on his walks to and from Oxford. After some years he persuaded the Fellows of Oriel College to provide the land for a church to be built. They also contributed towards the cost, and Newman's mother laid the foundation stone on 21 July 1835. Mrs Newman lived at Littlemore at the end of her life with her two daughters, Jemima and Harriet, but after her death and their marriages, Newman contented himself with lodgings once again. Having built the church, it was his constant ambition to obtain or build a parsonage. It took several years for this to happen and the achievement took an unusual form.

By April 1840 Newman had formed tentative plans to reside permanently at Littlemore. He told himself that there was as much pastoral work to do in the village as there was in the main part of his parish in Oxford itself, although he had no intention of abandoning St Mary's or his Oriel Fellowship. He wrote to Pusey discussing a revival of an earlier plan of Newman's for 'a monastic house . . . and coming up to live in it myself'.[21] Newman acquired some disused stables and a barn which he converted into a series of cottages with a library. They were linked by a wooden shed which was soon referred to as a cloister. Eventually a room was turned into a tiny oratory. As his disillusionment with the Church of England, with Oxford and with Oriel College grew, his affection for Littlemore developed and he used his premises as a refuge for himself and for various younger friends. Part of his motive at first had been to provide a facility that might retain within the Church of England some of the more advanced Romanizing followers of the Tractarians. People came out from Oxford to see what was happening, having heard rumours of 'a nest of papists'. Many years later Newman could appreciate the absurdity of the situation:

One day when I entered my house I found a flight of undergraduates inside. Heads of Houses, as mounted patrols, walked their horses round those poor cottages. Doctors of Divinity dived into the hidden recesses ... and drew domestic conclusions from what they saw there.[22]

Newspaper reports said that the place was a monastery, and the long-suffering Bishop of Oxford wrote asking for a denial. Newman gave the Bishop the assurance which he sought, but nevertheless he used the Greek term *mone* to describe the nascent community. Newman wanted to concentrate on scholarly work and on his devotional life. In a letter written at the end of March 1842, he said, he was 'setting up a half College half monastery at Littlemore', although he was alone there at the time.

This was the situation when *Tract 90* provoked such an adverse reaction. As we have seen, Newman was aghast at the turn of events. He was resident at Littlemore from April 1842, and it was natural that he should find refuge in a place that he had fitted up as a retreat. His extensive library had been moved there early in the same year. He was joined by like-minded individuals, the first of whom was J. D. Dalgairns, an immature young man who later converted to Roman Catholicism. A frequent visitor was the philosopher W. G. Ward who was a don at Balliol College. After his conversion to Roman Catholicism and his marriage, he lived nearby. In 1843 Ambrose St John arrived on a short visit. He was aged 28 and so was rather older than many of the others. He had doubts about the Church of England and also converted. He became Newman's closest friend until his death, effectively filling the position left long before by Hurrell Froude. In 1890 Newman was buried in St John's grave. A catastrophe arrived in the person of William Lockhart. Newman accepted him because his family feared that he would convert to Rome and it was thought that a stay at Littlemore would give him some stability. In Liddon's biography of Pusey there is an exchange of letters with Newman dated August 1842 which almost certainly refers to Lockhart. He is not named, but later references in the same volume confirm his identity.[23] Pusey wrote on behalf of 'a person for whom it really was worth asking'. He asked, among other things, whether Newman did not agree that the use of the Roman Breviary at Littlemore was unsettling for the young man. Newman replied rather testily that, despite a recent crisis, all was now well. Lockhart had promised to remain for three years, but left early in order to become a Roman Catholic in August 1843. This happened suddenly and was a shock to Newman. By his action, Lockhart precipitated the final crisis at Littlemore.

Despite these conversions and with others threatened among his friends and visitors, Newman continued to vacillate. He told J. B. Mozley that he could not continue to hold preferment in the Church of England. 'The truth is . . . I love the Church of Rome too well.'[24] Eventually he resigned his living in September 1843 in a letter to Bagot. His spiritual and theological uncertainty continued. He set out to clear his mind by using his pen, and began to write his *Essay on the Development of Christian Doctrine*. He hoped to publish it as an Anglican, but before it came out his mind was made up. The book's 'Advertisement', or preface, was dated 6 October 1845. The book had a very significant 'postscript' in which Newman wrote, 'Since the above was written the Author has joined the Roman Church. It was his intention and wish to have carried his volume through the press before deciding finally on this step.' But he had reached his conclusion before the publication date and 'circumstances gave him the opportunity of acting on it, and he felt that he had no warrant for refusing to act on it'.

On 25 September 1845 he preached his final sermon as an Anglican in the little church at Littlemore. Poignantly, he called it 'The Parting of Friends'. Many of his friends and collaborators were present, including Pusey. On 3 October he sent his resignation to the Provost of Oriel without an explanation. Around that time, Dalgairns and St John were received into the Roman Church. A few days later John Henry Newman faded from the history of the Oxford Movement. He was received into the Roman Catholic Church on 9 October, and went on to continue his illustrious ministry. Pusey was devastated, but tried to put a positive gloss on what Dean Church was later to call 'the catastrophe'. In a letter published in the *English Churchman* Pusey said, 'He seems then to me not so much gone from us, as transplanted into another part of the vineyard.'[25] Not everyone put such a charitable gloss on what Newman had done. It was to be 20 years before he met Pusey and Keble again, and he did not revisit Oxford until 1877.

Chapter 6

'The leaders stood firm'[1]

Newman's secession was incomparably the most significant of all those which took place at about that time. He was the only one of the authors of the *Tracts for the Times* to convert to Roman Catholicism in 1845. So severe was the shock of his going, although it had been long expected, that it took the informal collection of individuals who formed the Oxford Movement a long time to recover. There were a number of reasons for this. One was that men who had been colleagues suddenly found that they had to choose between friends and the Church which had nurtured them. A second was that those who had converted felt the need to persuade others to join them. Because they knew intimately the Church of England, converts were able to attack its weak points. As a result, many Anglo-Catholics felt beleaguered. This was further exacerbated by the attitude of the authorities of the Church of England, which appeared, as Dean Church thought, to be saying sternly to unsettled men that they should go; whilst simultaneously the Church of Rome seemed to be beckoning and welcoming.

In the 12 years since the appearance of the first of the *Tracts for the Times*, and since Keble had preached his Assize Sermon, the Movement had spread far beyond Oxford, but Newman had been the dominant force. His qualities of leadership were well known. He was a renowned preacher; his *Parochial and Plain Sermons* were published in eight volumes and had sold well. His sermons were very influential at the time of being preached and in their published form. Many people expressed a sense of indebtedness to them, not least Mrs Pusey and her daughter Lucy. His other theological writings also attracted much attention. In particular his own contributions to the *Tracts for the Times*, although notionally anonymous, had been widely read. His involvement in the Movement at every level meant that it was associated with his personality, even after the weight of Pusey's name, great learning and piety was added. The years at Littlemore, with the sense of a loss of direction, emphasized this phenomenon. It did not fade until well after Pusey had taken on the role of leader. The loss of Newman shifted the focus.

In the days before he began to change his mind, Newman had often fiercely denounced the Roman Church. Pusey and Keble had not used such emphatic language, although neither had been afraid to criticize. It was ironic that the comparatively moderate tones of Pusey and Keble were taken as evidence of their unsoundness as Anglicans. There were some, however, who were willing to trust them. In September 1845, a few weeks before Newman converted but at the time of high tension, Pusey received a letter from Benjamin Harrison. Despite the coolness which had followed Isaac Williams' failure over the Poetry Professorship, Harrison was a friend as well as a former pupil, assistant lecturer in Hebrew and a contributor to the *Tracts for the Times*. Pusey's biographer speculated that the letter was inspired by the anxiety of Archbishop Howley, as Harrison was his chaplain. In reply Pusey wrote frankly, as if to Harrison alone but with an eye to any other readers of the correspondence. 'I can only take the positive ground of love and duty to our own Church.' He could not provide condemnatory material about Rome, although he was aware of the difficulties faced by 'persons who are really in any risk of leaving us'. His own 'practical line . . . would be much as heretofore, to teach whatever Antiquity teaches as being herein in the line of our Church, and to try to promote practical holiness, leaving the result to God . . .'.[2]

There were undoubtedly many who thought that the secession of Newman would bring to an end the whole attempt to reassert the catholic credentials of the Church of England, and there were some who hoped that it would be so. Some opponents thought that all who shared the Tractarians' views would follow Newman. In fact the number of secessions was not large, although the figures were significant. William Palmer of Worcester College, writing in 1883, believed the total to have been about 50 clergymen. Recent research by G. Herring suggests that 40 is a more accurate estimate.[3] Palmer observed that there were approximately 20,000 clergy in the Church of England at the time. Among the opponents of the Movement, those who believed allegations about secret ambitions for reunion with Rome rejoiced at the secessions as clearing away traitors and cleansing the Church. Such men expected that those who remained would either see the error of their ways or be cowed into silence by the march of events.

For the Movement to survive the recent catastrophic events, it was clear that a new start was needed, but few could see how that could happen. The surviving Tractarians were demoralized, and some were close to despair, although this should not be exaggerated. It was natural for the Movement's adherents to look to Keble and Pusey for leadership, but Keble and Pusey were reluctant to lead and each of them denied that it was his calling to do so. Keble was at Hursley preoccupied with domestic anxieties and parish work, almost temperamentally disinclined to engage in a wider public life. His wife was recovering from severe illness, and his worries were increased because his brother was also unwell in his parish at Bisley. Although both recovered, Keble had feared for their lives at the time. Consequently he was of little use or support to Pusey. The two did not communicate immediately, but from the time of Newman's departure became closer in their friendship. Compelled as he was to remain at Hursley, Keble was helpless. His almost chronic modesty and genuine humility made him disinclined to take any active part in the unfolding events. He began a letter to Newman on 3 October, but did not finish it. When he returned to it on 11 October, it was after 'the thunderbolt [had] actually fallen upon us'. He seems to have concentrated entirely on his local responsibilities and to have simply waited upon God with regard to the Oxford situation. Certainly, that is borne out by an observation made by Newman many years later, and Walter Lock's biography of Keble provides the evidence. Lock quoted from an unpublished note which Newman attached to a bundle of material deposited in the library of Keble College:

> the idea had grown upon him [Keble] . . . that he had allowed himself for the last ten or twelve years to be engaged in deep religious questions, and in controversy arising out of them, without adequate preparation. He had set off in the company or at the head of many others, on a road which he had not explored, and as he might think, he had been 'the blind leading the blind'.[4]

Newman even thought that Keble might have blamed himself for his friend's conversion. This opinion would account for Keble's attitude, but R. W. Church disputed its accuracy and added his own comment which was dated 10 November 1879: 'in all his griefs he never lost his head or his faith; though if anything could have made him do so, it would have been the event of 1845 and the parting with Newman'.[5] A few years later, in the middle of another controversy, Keble made a statement which described, in very positive terms, his state of mind at the time of Newman's departure: 'if the Church of England were to fail, it should be found in my parish'.[6]

It was thought that Pusey would remain silent and reclusive with his books. Undergraduates were warned by their tutors and others to stay away from his house. He was still suffering as a result of the personal tragedies of his wife's death in 1839 and of his daughter's in 1844. He was further weighed down by the loss of Newman, for he knew that the rupture in relations had to be absolute. The debacle surrounding Ward's departure increased his gloom. However, the mantle of leadership unavoidably fell upon him. Oxford was the centre of the storm, and it was where Pusey continued to live and work. There was also the common and long standing reference to the whole group as 'Puseyites'. Pusey always denied that he was the leader of the Anglo-Catholics. Indeed, he denied that he even wanted to be a leader, and in the past had intervened only at moments when he thought doctrinal matters were at stake.[7] There is plenty of evidence of his apparent reluctance, but it comes from Pusey himself and has been largely accepted at face value. His assertions were, however, disputed by one of his contemporaries. William Palmer had written his *Narrative* in 1843, but he revised it in 1883 with an eight-chapter 'Introduction' and four chapters of 'Supplement'. Palmer, who had developed antipathy towards Newman, was unequivocal in his conviction that Pusey deliberately adopted the role of a leader in Newman's place. 'Immediately upon Newman's secession, and the collapse of the Romanizing party', he wrote, 'Pusey threw himself into the breach and published letters announcing himself as the leader of the Tractarian movement.'[8] Palmer was not entirely happy with what he perceived to be Pusey's new role: 'I must confess that Pusey's proceedings as the self-constituted leader of the Tractarian party often caused me very great uneasiness.' His anxieties, however, were doctrinal. He thought that Pusey was too conciliatory towards those of 'Romanizing views'. He did not dispute the appropriateness of Pusey taking the role of leader.

The fact that Pusey decided to speak in the form of a public letter broke the barrier and made it possible for the process which had begun with the *Tracts for the Times* to continue in a new and different manner. The letter was written with the express intention that it should be a public document, and it appeared in the *English Churchman* of 16 October 1845. Following Newman's bombshell, Pusey's letter was the most significant immediate response and catapulted him at once into the leadership role. It was addressed to an unnamed 'Dear Friend' and the addressee was fictional. This was a literary device which enabled Pusey to write frankly and informally and to avoid a tone of oversight. The idea was that he should not appear to be a leader addressing his party, although that is what he was. Many assumed that the intended recipient was Keble, but it is known that the two had not been in touch since before Newman left. The letter was long, and worked from an acknowledgement of the pain of separation, which he recognized as a 'chastisement', through to a degree of hopefulness for the Church of England. This was his considered opinion, reflecting on 'these last ten years, [and, indeed] a yet longer period'. This 'hopefulness' was because of 'God's Holy Spirit dwelling in our Church, vouchsafed through His ordinances, teaching us to value them more deeply, to seek them more habitually, to draw fresh life from them'. That, he claimed, was a work by God and a development that would not have been given to any Church which God 'purposed to leave'. So God 'will surely not forsake us now'.[9] Pusey was effective in the letter because he sounded a quiet note of continuity and even confidence amid the anxiety. He had not written a ringing denunciation of Newman and his move, nor of Rome. Keble wrote at once to commend him for the letter, which he had read for the first time in the journal, and claimed to feel as if he had received it as a personal communication. It was a judicious and timely contribution by a man who, whatever his self-distrust and consequent failure to give a lead on other occasions, had genuine qualities of leadership.

With Pusey's emergence as the leader, a steadying force became dominant. Despite Newman's hopes that his friend would follow him to Rome, Pusey stood firm and did not doubt the validity of the Church of England. He was distressed at the Church's shortcomings, but he never shared Newman's fears that it was fundamentally a heretical body. He believed that it was theologically damaged and only partially represented the ancient catholic faith; but they were reasons to fight for it, not to give it up. When Newman's powerful personality was removed, men realized that there was another anchor holding the Movement in place in the person of Dr Pusey. He was an anchor that would not fail and had been there all the time, but his strength had been largely unnoticed. Pusey's supporters and biographers were anxious to present him as undoubting and firm in his adherence to the Church of England. He was certainly shaken by the conversion of one of his closest collaborators and friends, but he held to his own perception of Church principles and always believed that Newman was grievously mistaken in his action. Life under Pusey's leadership looked as though it would be less volatile and more considered. His concern was different from Newman's in that he wanted to mend the Church so that it could serve God and fulfil its tasks; Newman had been worried about whether it was a Church at all. Pusey, with Keble's support and that of their colleagues who remained, turned the Movement in a new direction. It ceased to be one man's show, although it had never really been that, and looked to all its friends and supporters to do the work. The clue to the next phase lay in a statement in Pusey's letter in the *English Churchman*, 'that the work which [God] has been carrying on is not with individuals, but with the Church as a whole'.[10]

Under the new leadership, Pusey hoped and expected that God would continue that work. He knew that it would be done by the Church through the human agency of its clergy and people working together. Over the years, many men had left Oxford after taking their degrees, and many of them had gone to serve as curates. A good proportion of them, and of those who had left the University but not been ordained, had been disciples of the Tractarians and so the influence of the Oxford Movement was already well diffused throughout the country. At a more senior level, clerical dons who were adherents of the Movement had also gone from Oxford into college incumbencies and in their pastoral work had carried forward the Tractarian ideals. Others who were not former students or dons had also felt the attraction of Oxford Movement principles and they were added to the numbers that were already significant. It is sufficient at this point to recall that the Tractarians were not without friends in the Church of England at large. Keble, with his parochial devotion, is an obvious example of a parish clergyman for whom the principles were all-important. So too was his brother Tom, the vicar of Bisley. Frederick Oakeley, the friend and associate of W. G. Ward, was in charge of the Margaret Street chapel in the west end of London until his secession, but Tractarian principles continued to be applied in the working of the area after Oakeley left. Some clues as to the extent of Tractarian influence can be found in a lengthy article by W. J. Conybeare in the *Edinburgh Review* of October 1853. In the section devoted to the 'High Church party', he struck at what he perceived to be the follies of the followers of the Tractarians, and almost incidentally revealed that there were significant numbers of such men. The last part of his article was an attempt to ascertain the relative strength of the parties within the Church of England. This endeavour was, to say the least, imprecise. He went through the *Clergy List*, which contained about 18,000 names, rather fewer than Palmer had estimated, and assessed about 500 'whose opinions we knew'. Conybeare then extrapolated from that figure and concluded that of 8,000 High Church clergy about 1,000 could be called Tractarian. This compared with totals of 6,500 Low Church and 3,500 whom he categorized as Broad Church. A similar figure to Conybeare's is given by Herring,[11] but he maintained that this number was spread across the period 1840–1870.

It is difficult to assess the number of clergy who might be called Tractarians, and there has sometimes been a tendency to confuse them with old-fashioned High Churchmen to whom some of the Tractarian theories appealed. It has already been shown that there was some degree of High Church revival before the Oxford men began their agitation, and this complicates any assessment. Although there is a paucity of information about the spread of Tractarianism beyond Oxford 'before about 1860',[12] it would be a mistake to assume that the Movement was without followers in parishes and other institutions. The Oxford Tracts had been received with interest by many, as the early sales indicated. A. P. Perceval helped to produce *The Churchman's Manual* soon after the Hadleigh Conference. He claimed that it was 'the first Tract' and asserted that its object 'was to supply a defect in the public instruction of the Church'.[13] The devotional manuals which Pusey later translated, adapted and published also helped to spread catholic principles. The Movement's first chroniclers understandably concentrated almost exclusively on the Oxford men and their activities and largely ignored the wider world. Further, the Movement soon became associated with ritualism, which probably could not have happened without it, and this also clouded the picture with regard to the extent of the spread of the intellectual and theological ideals of the initial instigators. The development of ritualism and its relation to the original Tractarians is extremely important and will be considered in the next chapter.

An influential priest who conducted his ministry along lines that the Oxford men found to be congenial was W. F. Hook, who was vicar of Leeds from 1837 to 1859. Although they had been friends in the early days, Hook and Pusey were estranged for many years. The problem arose over the church of St Saviour which was built in

Hook's parish. The money for it was provided by an anonymous sinner anxious for God's forgiveness. There was to be an inscription asking all who entered to pray for the sinner who was the donor. The Bishop of Ripon, C. T. Longley, was worried about consecrating the place because he feared that the donor might be deceased, and he did not approve of prayers for the dead. There was an exchange of correspondence in which Pusey admitted that the donor was still alive, and he was forced to promise to notify the Bishop when the donor died. In fact, Pusey was the donor, but this was never disclosed because he survived the Bishop. The intention was to provide a place of worship where the principles of the Oxford Movement could be carried into practice. The plan was for a celibate group of clergy to work in a Leeds slum which had lacked a church building of its own. Pusey pretended to act as the intermediary, and all the correspondence and financial arrangements were made through him. A chalice, enriched by Lucy Pusey's jewels, was provided as a memorial of her. The church was a very early example of 'Victorian gothic' and the principles of the Cambridge Camden Society (which became the Ecclesiological Society) were represented in its design by the involvement of Benjamin Webb.

The consecration took place just a fortnight after Newman's secession. Hook had become apprehensive about the event. He feared that the new church would be 'filled with scoffing Methodists'. The problems were to come later and were to do with the matter of secessions to Rome. In its early years, St Saviour's, Leeds, saw a succession of its clergy convert to Roman Catholicism, more than any other parish in the country. The robust Hook blamed Pusey for recommending and sending the wrong men and was understandably annoyed. He said he had spent 10 years in the parish fighting for the Church of England 'against the Puritans, so will I now fight for her against the Romanisers'.[14] It was not until 1873, when Hook was Dean of Chichester, that the rift was healed on his initiative in a letter to Liddon. He conveyed Hook's message of reconciliation to Pusey who responded warmly and at once.[15]

One priest who served St Saviour's and who remained loyal to Anglicanism was A. P. Forbes, whom Pusey recommended in 1847. Unfortunately for Hook and Pusey, he only remained in the parish for a short time before being elected Bishop of Brechin. It was Forbes who took Tractarian principles to Scotland, for he continued at Brechin for the rest of his life, and became known as 'the Scottish Pusey'. His ministry was not without its detractors and he underwent censure from his fellow bishops in 1860 for his declared views on the Real Presence of Christ in the Eucharist. Nevertheless, he continued to proclaim the catholicity of Anglicanism in Scotland for a further 15 years.

As the Oxford Movement began to be a recognizable element within the life of the Church outside Oxford, so the bishops had to respond to the catholic-minded clergy in their dioceses. After the series of Episcopal Charges hostile to *Tract 90*, there was no likelihood of the bishops looking with favour upon such men. There were two exceptions to what appeared almost to be a rule. The first was Benjamin Harrison, an early enthusiast. He wrote *Tract 16*, *Tract 17*, *Tract 24* and *Tract 49*. He was appointed domestic chaplain, and also an examining chaplain, to Archbishop Howley in 1838. In this post, as has been noted, he had to tread carefully, but it did mean that the Tractarians had a sympathetic ear close to the Archbishop of Canterbury. In 1845 he became Archdeacon of Maidstone and a Residentiary Canon of Canterbury Cathedral until his death in 1887.

The second notable promotion was Walter Kerr Hamilton. He was the first of the followers of the Oxford Movement to become a diocesan bishop. Having been educated in Oxford, he had come under the influence of the Tractarians whilst serving as a parish clergyman in Oxford. Initially the attraction of the Movement for Hamilton was its call to live a holy life.[16] In 1841 he became a Canon of Salisbury and then bishop of the diocese in 1854 where he remained for the rest of his life.

The preferments of these two able Tractarian clergymen were sufficiently rare events to merit notice. But other experienced clergy felt themselves to be excluded from preferment of even the most modest kind. Some young men with Tractarian sympathies experienced difficulty in obtaining ordination. One of the worst cases of discrimination in the early days had been that of Peter Young, Keble's long-suffering curate. John Mason Neale provides an example of a young and able priest who was excluded from the normal run of clerical careers. Neale was something of a firebrand, and never held a benefice. As an undergraduate he had been one of the founders of the Cambridge Camden Society, an organization which did much to promote interest in ecclesiastical architecture and ritual and helped to promote the gothic revival in Victorian Britain. For many years he was the Warden of some almshouses in East Grinstead. For 16 years he was formally inhibited from exercising his priestly functions in the Diocese of Chichester by the Bishop, A. T. Gilbert, who in the days of the

Tracts was Principal of Brasenose College, Oxford, and so one of the Heads of House. It was from his almshouses that Neale poured his prodigious stream of books, pamphlets and translations and compositions of hymns. Neale is also important because in 1854 he founded a nursing sisterhood, the Society of St Margaret.

The idea of reviving religious orders had occurred to Pusey many years before as a means of encouraging holiness of life. It had been his and his daughter Lucy's ambition from an early age that she should dedicate herself to such a life, but she died at the age of 15. A. M. Allchin identified three factors that influenced the founders of religious orders in the nineteenth-century Church of England.[17] First, and important to Pusey, was the monasticism of the patristic period. Next, was the influence of medieval monasticism which, in the popular mind, was thought to be the most significant. This accorded with the gothic revival in architecture, and with Romanticism in popular and serious literature in the middle of the century. The third category, however, is one that was largely overlooked at the time but this was the inspiration which a number of the founders, Pusey and Neale among them, drew from the active orders which had been founded in the seventeenth century. Neale went to France and Belgium and visited such communities in his desire for information and ideas. Pusey had made similar visits to communities in Ireland in the summer vacation of 1841.

It was at Pusey's hands that the concept was transformed into a reality. Marion Rebecca Hughes, like the young Lucy Pusey, was attracted to the idea of greater holiness of life by Newman's sermons. On 5 June 1841, Trinity Sunday, she took religious vows of poverty, chastity and obedience privately in the presence of Pusey. She was 23 years old. Later that same day she received Holy Communion from Newman in St Mary's church, Oxford, with Lucy Pusey kneeling beside her. She is thought to be the first person within the Church of England to take such vows since the Reformation. Like many Victorian young women she was subject to the rule of her parents and it was not until 1849, after they had both died, that she was free to follow publicly the way of life to which she was called. Eventually she became the Superior of the Convent of the Holy Trinity in Oxford, one of several communities that functioned in the Oxford Diocese under the tolerant eye of Bishop Samuel Wilberforce.

The first religious community was in London, near to Regent's Park, and started with four women at Park Village West. Bishop Blomfield of London was uneasy and advised against the little community but later changed his mind. The sisters ran an orphanage and a school for poor children and also visited slum areas. One of the adherents of the Tractarians was W. J. Butler, the vicar of Wantage. He had investigated sisterhoods in France and established a small community in his parish. Within a few years it had begun to specialize in the care of unmarried mothers and in seeking to rescue prostitutes from their way of life. Pusey was directly involved in the establishment of a community set up with the encouragement of Bishop Phillpotts of Exeter. He persuaded Priscilla Lydia Sellon to abandon plans to leave the country and serve as a missionary. Instead, she set up a sisterhood which worked among the poverty-stricken inhabitants of Plymouth and Devonport. A few years later when the Park Village community was at a low ebb, Miss Sellon's sisterhood, which by then had branches elsewhere in the west country, took over its work and assimilated its surviving members. The Sisterhood of St Margaret, founded by John Mason Neale, also cared for the poor and destitute and, within a few years, had widened its work to include orphanages and schools. Many other communities were founded, the great majority of them for women, often in the teeth of Protestant hostility. Some were very short-lived, but others became respected elements of the life of the Church of England.

Neale had written a poor novel, *Ayton Priory, or the Restored Monastery*, in 1843. In it he dreamed of the re-establishment of a religious community on land and in buildings that had been alienated at the Dissolution. He imagined them to be occupied by a community of men. It was not until 1865, however, that the first stable community for men was founded in the Church of England. This was the Society of St John the Evangelist, and its founder was Richard Meux Benson, the vicar of Cowley just outside Oxford. He was inspired to establish the community as a result of Keble's preaching, not by Neale's novel. The society won respect and eventually worked beyond the confines of England. Among other communities for men, the Society of the Sacred Mission was founded by Herbert Kelly in 1891, and the Community of the Resurrection was created by Charles Gore in 1892. It was the sisterhoods that came first and inevitably they were regarded as 'popish' in the early years and had to struggle to overcome prejudice. Neale, for example, encountered a great deal of hostility and his house was attacked by an arsonist. Later he and several sisters had to flee from a hostile mob after attending a sister's funeral in Lewes in Sussex.

It was in 1847 that a fresh controversy occurred and challenged the hard-won stability which the Tractarians were beginning to achieve after the secessions. This time they found that they had allies else-where in the Church and in national life. It all began when an obscure country clergyman of Calvinistic views secured a living in Devonshire, a village called Brampford Speke, which was in the gift of the Lord Chancellor. He was the Reverend George Cornelius Gorham and was already serving in the Exeter Diocese, which then included Cornwall. The Bishop was Henry Phillpotts, a tough-minded and fearless old-fashioned High Churchman, who enjoyed a battle and was already uneasy about Gorham. He disapproved of Gorham's theological position and subjected him to a lengthy and gruelling examination concerning the doctrine of baptism, and found him wanting. In brief, Gorham did not accept the declared doctrine of the Book of Common Prayer that upon baptism a person, whether child or adult, is regenerated or 'born again' through the sacrament. Bishop Phillpotts therefore refused to institute Gorham to the new parish. Gorham was as combative as the bishop, and challenged Phillpotts' decision. He resorted to the courts and eventually the issue became, for the High Churchmen, more a matter of authority and jurisdiction than the permissible doctrine of baptism which was the cause of the litigation. Since the publicity over *Tract 90* many churchmen were anxious about the extent of liberty of belief. Gorham was claiming the same freedom, although for Protestant opinions, as Newman and Ward had demanded for catholic views. The Tractarians were particularly interested in a controversy that revolved around the two doctrines of the sacraments and the authority of the Church in the person of a bishop. Pusey followed the case with interest, not least because of his work on baptism for the Tracts. The question was not merely one that concerned the Oxford Movement men and their followers. Many High Churchmen feared that their position would become impossible if Phillpotts were to be defeated. Conversely, evangelicals who thought that Gorham was right feared that they would not be able to stay in the Church of England if their views were held to be inadmissible. The liberals were once again anxious that definitions should be avoided.

In June 1848 Gorham asked the Court of Arches to overrule the Bishop and compel him to institute him to the parish. The Court of Arches was the ancient consistory court of the Province of Canterbury and was the most senior ecclesiastical court to which Gorham could appeal. It was presided over by the Dean of the Court of Arches, Sir Herbert Jenner Fust. The Court examined the case carefully by looking at the doctrine of baptism in the Early Fathers, the Reformers of the sixteenth century and in Anglican writings. Two years after Gorham had been offered the parish, Fust delivered his judgement in early August 1849. The judge upheld the Bishop, and Gorham immediately looked elsewhere for a remedy.

He turned to the Judicial Committee of the Privy Council, which since 1833 had been the final court of appeal for ecclesiastical matters. The two Archbishops and Bishop Blomfield of London were the ecclesiastical members of the Committee and the remainder were laymen. It was the first time that the Judicial Committee had been asked to examine a doctrinal matter. Its authority to do so had not been previously considered because such a question had not arisen. Because of the lay majority, High Churchmen were anxious that the Committee should not deal with a doctrinal question, on the grounds that the majority of the judges were not competent to do so. This anxiety turned the matter from being simply a question of the soundness of Gorham's views into a question of the relationship between the Church of England and the state. The question had become double-edged as far as the High Churchmen were concerned. First, there was the matter of whether the Church of England's doctrine of baptismal regeneration was as defined in the Book of Common Prayer and the Catechism. Second, where did Anglican authority lie, in the bishops or in a predominately lay tribunal? Coleridge told Pusey that the Committee could be defended by the claim that it was constituted to deal with the temporal consequences of decisions such as Phillpotts had made. Pusey replied at length and corresponded with Keble on this point.

When judgement was given in March 1850, Gorham was triumphant. The Judicial Committee declared, in the face of the Prayer Book baptism service and the Catechism, that the Church's doctrine of baptismal regeneration was not explicitly defined. High Churchmen were dismayed. Phillpotts protested vigorously. He also suffered a private humiliation at about this time. His chaplain, a liturgical scholar named Maskell, converted to Roman Catholicism. He had some prior warning, and told Pusey what to expect. Pusey was in touch with Keble who wondered whether Gorham could be prosecuted for heresy, but the suggestion was soon abandoned. The implication of the judgement for those of a catholic cast of mind was stark. The Committee had declared that the Church of England did not hold a doctrine which its supporters believed to be essential to catholic theological integrity. For the Tractarians it seemed that Committee was denying the Church one of its fundamental doctrines.

Immediately steps were taken to overturn the judgement, but nothing could be done at a level higher than that of objection. Bishops received protests from individual laity and clergy and from groups. A meeting was called for 23 July in St Martin's Hall, Longacre, and 1,500 attended. It was necessary to hold an overflow meeting in the nearby Freemasons Tavern. Pusey spoke at the latter, which was under the chairmanship of Lord Fielding. The organizers suggested that there should be no applause and so the meetings had the air of 'a solemn synodical assembly'.[18] Several documents were adopted by the meeting. One was simply headed 'Protest'. Another was a petition to the Queen and a third, which was handed to Archbishop Sumner at Lambeth two days later, was addressed to the English bishops. The pamphlet war that had broken out early in the case continued and around 60 publications eventually appeared, with each side stating its case with force.

The Gorham case had some unexpected consequences. One was that it gave added impetus to the campaign for the restoration of the Convocations of Canterbury and York in order that each could perform its proper function in the government of the Church. The desire to reinstate Convocation had grown since the Reform Act of 1832 and its eventual revival was a most significant change in the relationship between the Church and the state following that Act. As an Anglican, Newman had written about the need for Convocation in the *British Magazine*. Apart from very brief, formal and highly infrequent meetings, Convocation had been suspended since 1717. It was, however, the nearest thing that the Church of England had to self-government. It was an entirely clerical body, consisting of two Houses. The Upper House was the bishops, and the Lower House was made up of elected clergy and a large number of dignitaries who were *ex officio* members.

Many evangelicals, such as Shaftesbury and Archbishop Sumner, were opposed to reviving Convocation, as were the liberals and those who were untroubled by fears about Parliament's ascendancy over the Church, which is known as erastianism. The evangelicals shared the fears of the theological liberals that an active Convocation might reduce the degree of liberty of belief. Sumner also had a practical objection that the membership would divide along party lines and become unmanageable. The idea that Convocation should be revived found its strongest proponents among High Churchmen. The Tractarians and their followers hoped to see an active Convocation as at least a partial answer to the erastianism which they believed to compromise the catholic doctrine of the Church. Gladstone was a keen supporter of the suggestion, but he wanted there to be a distinct involvement of laymen. Pusey heard that Gladstone was about to produce a pamphlet urging lay involvement and wrote a letter in which he tried to stop him. The idea of laymen helping in the government of the Church was unacceptable to men like Pusey and Keble, and to old-style High Churchmen such as Bishop Phillpotts. They recognized that Convocation should properly be concerned with matters of doctrine and believed that the laity were not competent to handle such matters. Phillpotts, in a letter to Pusey, expressed himself succinctly on the matter of the theological competence of the laity, 'very few . . . can be deemed sound or orthodox'.[19]

The process by which Convocation regained a meaningful existence and gave the clergy a voice was lengthy. The Convocation of Canterbury was finally re-established in 1852, but that of York had to wait. In 1860 the Archbishop of York, Musgrave, died. He had been utterly opposed to the revival and had prevented it meeting. His successor Longley immediately allowed it to meet, which it did for the first time in 1861. The laity had to wait for a voice in Church government until the Enabling Act of 1919.

As the Gorham case faded from the public memory, another piece of litigation took its place. It was less notorious than Gorham, but just as dangerous to the Tractarian concept of Christian orthodoxy. The unfortunate Bishop Bagot, now translated to Bath and Wells from Oxford, was involved. The protagonist was one of his own Archdeacons, G. A. Denison of Taunton, who had been a Fellow of Oriel with Keble and Pusey. Rather like Bishop Phillpotts, he was a man who enjoyed a fight and it is thought that Anthony Trollope modelled Archdeacon Grantly on Denison. He was a High Churchman, but not a committed Tractarian, yet had outspoken views on the sacraments. He demanded that ordination candidates eschewed the views of men like Gorham, and he preached a series of fiercely dogmatic sermons on the Eucharist in Wells cathedral. A foolhardy man, he tried to provoke a prosecution for his views and eventually succeeded. Keble and Pusey were concerned was that, if Denison were condemned, then the Tractarian understanding of the sacraments would be lost. Keble wrote to the *Guardian*, a High Church weekly, which succinctly expressed the difficulty. If Denison's opinions were 'declared untenable in the Church of England, a far more serious question would arise concerning the reality of our communion with the Universal Church than has yet arisen'.[20] Pusey also entered the fray with 'notes' to his sermon on the Eucharist. The notes were a substantial volume of 700 pages and had the title, *The Real Presence in the Fathers*. Keble wrote his *On Eucharistical Adoration*, which was published in 1857, and in the same year Pusey added to the corpus with a shorter book. Its title can be summarized as *The Real Presence . . . the Doctrine of the English Church*. Denison had courageous supporters, and yet was condemned and deprived of his preferment until a higher court overturned the judgement. The case dragged on until 1858 until it was dismissed by the Judicial Committee of the Privy Council.

Although feelings were bruised by the outcome of the Denison case, some Anglicans had been utterly dismayed by the Gorham disaster and they felt they could no longer remain in the Church of England. On 6 April 1851 Henry Manning, the Archdeacon of Chichester, became the second and, apart from Newman, the only contributor to the *Tracts for the Times* to convert to Roman Catholicism. Keble had been anxious about Manning at the time of Newman's secession and had tried to help him then. Pusey had written often to Manning as the Gorham case developed. Manning's name appeared at the top of a list of High Churchmen who signed the protest. Pusey and Keble also signed, but they remained in the Church of England and provided much-needed stability for the surviving majority of the Oxford Movement men. Another important secession was that of Robert Isaac Wilberforce, Manning's brother-in-law, a son of the great William Wilberforce and brother of Samuel the Bishop of Oxford. He lingered as Archdeacon of the East Riding of Yorkshire until 1854, but it was the Gorham case which destroyed his adherence to the Church of England. When he converted, he went to Paris to do so, in order to save his episcopal brother from embarrassment. Another of the Wilberforce brothers, Henry, also converted, but did so in England. Another notable secession was Lord Fielding. He had been chairman of the overflow meeting on 23 July 1850, and went soon afterwards. There were a number of other secessions. The numbers were greater than had been the case after *Tract 90*. Herring thought that 56 clergy went in the period 1850–1854.[21] Keble and Pusey disappointed Manning by remaining in the Church of England.

It was the Gorham case that caused Keble to make his remark about the Church surviving in his parish even if it failed elsewhere. Keble had long doubted the usefulness of the Church's established status and the Gorham case did nothing to make him change his mind. Indeed, at times it almost seemed that he hoped for an adverse outcome because it would strengthen his argument for disestablishment.[22] When the case went against the Bishop, Keble spoke warmly of the non-jurors who, over a century before, had relinquished their places in the Church rather than submit to the new constitutional arrangements after 1688. Phillpotts was of a practical cast of mind and had no doubts. He still refused to institute Gorham and threatened to excommunicate anyone who did install him in the parish. This was a veiled threat to Archbishop Sumner, but it did not deter him and Gorham was installed in his parish in August 1850 by Fust who acted under a *fiat* of the Archbishop.

Another consequence of the Gorham debacle was a chain of events which Gorham himself could not have predicted and which would have been abhorrent to him. Nicholas Wiseman, who was now the Roman Catholic Vicar Apostolic of the London District, called upon the Church of England to 'return to the bosom of the Catholic Church'.[23] Wiseman had been in Rome back in the days of the trip which Newman and Froude had made in 1833. He was an impatient man who at this point hoped to benefit from Anglican disarray. Although the case did not have a direct bearing on the situation, it and the subsequent secessions contributed to Nicholas Wiseman's belief that the time was ripe to establish a Roman Catholic hierarchy in England. It was an idea that had been gaining ground although, in the years following the Emancipation Acts, Roman Catholics had continued to be a subdued minority in England quietly living out their faith in more-or-less contented obscurity. In 1844 and in 1846 additional legislation had removed most of the outstanding legal disabilities which had not been dealt with by the Act of 1829. Both to the old-style Roman Catholics and to the enthusiasts such as Wiseman this was a source of encouragement. The Prime Minister was Lord John Russell and he appointed his father-in-law, Lord Minto, ambassador to Rome.

Many of the converts from the Church of England in the 1840s had been Oxford intellectuals and did not fit easily into the Roman system. The conversion of Newman added to the new sense of optimism that Roman Catholics were feeling, but they did not know what to make of him. They did not like the thought that he had converted because of his disquiet at the Church of England rather than because of an enthusiasm for the Church he was joining. An additional problem arose in the 1840s when the famine in Ireland caused an influx of immigrants. The Roman Catholic bishops in England were known as Vicars Apostolic and were directly answerable to Rome as there was no hierarchy in England. They wanted more freedom of action and hoped that the establishment of a proper hierarchy would give it to them. The idea had been frustrated by the opposition of Cardinal Acton, who lived and worked in Rome. He wanted to maintain the existing arrangements whereby Rome directly managed and controlled English Roman Catholicism. The arrival of the Irish put an intolerable strain on the Vicars Apostolic and their clergy. For a long time Wiseman had nursed an ambition to take the step of setting up a hierarchy. Acton died in 1847, a year after the election of a new Pope, Pius IX, and Wiseman saw his opportunity. A scheme was agreed in Rome in 1847, but it was not implemented until 1850. Rome had its own internal reasons to delay, but also considered the English situation and decided to wait until there was a Whig administration in England and then to act at a time when Parliament was in recess. Wiseman was ambitious for his Church and for himself. He was a clever man, but was blinded by his ambition and caused a national outcry by his timing and by his insensitivity.

The establishment of the Roman Catholic hierarchy led to a considerable controversy at all levels of English society. Wiseman claimed that both Russell and Minto had been informed in advance and had raised no objections. Both denied this, but it seems that discussions of some imprecise sort had taken place. Eventually 12 dioceses were set up, plus the Archdiocese of Westminster. The naming of them proved to be highly contentious. Rome and Wiseman decided to avoid the titles of the sees of the Church of England, and they were sensible to do so. Indeed, Parliament passed the Ecclesiastical Titles Act which prevented them from duplicating the names of Anglican dioceses, although later there was some duplication when the Church of England subsequently established additional new dioceses. As an Act of Parliament it proved to be unworkable and 20 years later was repealed when Gladstone was Prime Minister. Wiseman, who was created a cardinal by the Pope, was to be the Archbishop of Westminster. Although Westminster was not the name of a current see held by an English bishop, it proved to be contentious because of its association with the seat of government. Wiseman felt a sense of personal triumph at the outcome and allowed it to influence his behaviour. In addition to the grandeur of his lifestyle, he issued a 'Pastoral Letter'. For reasons of Roman Catholic protocol, it was published from the northern gate of the city of Rome, the 'Flaminian Gate'. He asserted that England was greatly blessed by the establishment of the Roman Catholic hierarchy, and his pastoral letter has been described as more of a manifesto or challenge to those who were not Roman Catholics than a pastoral letter to his flock.[24] This added to the English sense of outrage at what soon came to be called the 'Papal Aggression'.

Wiseman had fuelled the fire with his call for Anglicans to 'return' to Rome, and he made matters worse by persuading Newman to lecture publicly in London. Newman's Lectures on *Certain Difficulties Felt by Anglicans in Submitting to the Catholic Church* were not tactful. They were not meant to be, for they were an appeal to the Tractarians and their followers to convert. The situation served to emphasize the innate Protestantism of the ordinary people and this had an unfortunate backlash for the men of the Oxford Movement. Wiseman's activities made life more difficult for Pusey and his followers. A belligerent sermon by Newman, which was published as *Christ upon the Waters*, added to the sense of outrage and for a while England was ill-disposed towards the Church of Rome. Meetings were held all over the country, and not all the opposition was merely verbal. There was some violence shown to Roman Catholic clergy and members of religious orders and also towards some of the Church's property. Wiseman had incorrectly assumed that the old cries of 'no popery' would not be heard again. Liddon's measured tones said there was 'a fever of excitement, which now appears quite in excess of the provocation'.[25]

Wiseman always believed that the Tractarian movement would lead catholic-minded Anglicans into Roman Catholicism and he and his advisers expected that the setting up of the hierarchy would bring them large numbers of converts. Certainly after the Judicial Committee of the Privy Council gave its ruling on Gorham, the Church of England was an unhappy place. There was a tendency for followers of the Tractarians to be blamed for being leaders of the opposition to Gorham and the judgement. In a similar way they were blamed for the controversy that erupted over the actions of Wiseman and the authorities in Rome. The secular press lambasted them and the evangelical side of the religious press was equally outspoken in its blame of the Oxford men. The accusations that they were secret sympathizers and supporters of Roman Catholicism surfaced once again. This was unjust in the majority of cases, for those who were sympathetic to Rome had mostly seceded and the Tractarians who remained loyal Anglicans were as dismayed as any others at the 'Papal Aggression'. However, the Tractarians were the victims of many public speakers and journalists who sought to make capital out of religious prejudices. Pusey suffered some personal abuse and was described by a rustic as 'such a friend of the Pope'.[26] The reality was that both the Gorham case and the matter of the hierarchy were phenomena over which the Tractarians had no control or influence. When Manning was received into the Roman Church, Wiseman described him as 'one of the first-fruits of the restoration of the hierarchy'.[27] That was inaccurate: Manning had left because of what he perceived to be the ineluctable erastianism illustrated by the Judicial Committee of the Privy Council.

Chapter 7

'Ritualism and Ritual'[1]

It is safe to claim that the Tractarians were entirely consistent in holding a high doctrine of the sacraments as a corollary of their doctrine of the Church. Ritualism developed out of a desire by some of the Tractarians and their followers to demonstrate sacramental doctrine through the elaboration of ecclesiastical ceremonial. Although there were inevitably variations in the nature and extent of belief between individuals, the Tractarians' approach was to present the sacraments as objective realities. This was in accord with the Catechism in the Book of Common Prayer, which defined a sacrament as an 'outward and visible sign of an inward and spiritual grace, given unto us, ordained by Christ himself'. Pusey observed in a letter to the Reverend G. R. Prynne:

> I have long felt that we must win the hearts of the people, and then the fruits of reverence will show themselves. To begin with outward things seems like gathering flowers and putting them in the earth to grow. If we win their hearts, all the rest will follow.[2]

As is clear from this letter, Pusey was not greatly inclined to promote ritual practices in church services if they were not supported by thorough teaching beforehand. Eventually it became a source of distress to him that his name was linked with some of the worst excesses of the ritualists, for his desire for restraint was not accepted by all his followers, and not by Prynne among them. By the 1870s, however, Pusey had, in a limited way, modified his opinion about ritual and had adopted some of the practices which he had earlier eschewed. He always advised moderation and careful regard for the feelings of others and stood by his advice to Prynne to regard ritual as secondary to faithful teaching, preaching and pastoral work.

Within living memory it had been customary for the Holy Communion to be celebrated only infrequently in parish churches, although there had been a desire to improve this situation since the time of the Wesleys. High Churchmen of the old school had usually been content with a monthly celebration, the Tractarians struggled initially for a weekly, and eventually for a daily, celebration. As the sacramental theology of the Oxford Movement spread into the parishes, there came to be an increasing number of celebrations of the Eucharist along with a more conscientious observation of the obligations regarding Morning and Evening Prayer. Newman had claimed that his management of St Mary's, Oxford, was conservative, but he had introduced additional services. At Bisley there had been a similar development under the leadership of Tom Keble in adding to the number and frequency of celebrations of the Eucharist as well as the Daily Offices. Hook at Coventry, and later at Leeds, had been assiduous, and these examples merely reflect the practice of many other conscientious parish clergy. Almost simultaneously there began to be elaborations of the ceremonial of such services.

All of this could be inferred from the fundamental ideals of the Oxford Movement, although the founding fathers had not thought of it. Their appeal to the early Church and to the sixteenth-century Anglican divines encouraged others to look to the medieval period and the confidence with which the Church then conducted its liturgy. This linked, in secular life, with Romantic notions about the Middle Ages. During the 1830s and 1840s, as Nigel Yates has recently noticed in his *Anglican Ritualism in Victorian Britain*, there had been a considerable increase in interest in the past. When this came to be expressed in Church terms, it 'endeavoured to harness medievalism and romanticism to be of practical benefit to the ecclesiastical community'.[3] An additional factor which has to be remembered was the love of ornateness which many newly wealthy Victorians enjoyed. It was natural that they should wish to reflect that love in their places of worship. Gladstone pointed out that the wealthy were likely to have 'a preference for churches and for services with a certain amount of ornament'. This may simply be 'the demand of the richer man for a more costly article'.[4] Some Anglicans looked to the modern Roman Church for inspiration as the only contemporary model for advanced ritual. Such behaviour obviously appealed to those who had Romanizing inclinations but had not converted to Roman Catholicism. These elements did not meet with the approval of Keble or Pusey, so it was particularly ironic that the phenomenon of ritualism should continue to be known as 'Puseyism'.

Despite a lack of enthusiasm among the surviving founders of the Oxford Movement, ritualism grew in popularity. Frederick Oakeley had left Balliol and was working in London. He was in charge of the Margaret Street chapel, which was later to be replaced by the famous Butterfield designed church of All Saints, until with Ward he went over to Rome. He had the rare gift, said Gladstone, 'of discerning and expressing the harmony between the inward purposes of Christian worship and its outward investiture'.[5] Oakeley regarded ritual precision as important for the proper expression of a reverent attitude. Dean Church described Oakeley as

> perhaps, the first to realise the capacities of the Anglican ritual for impressive devotional use, and his services [and also] his chapel, are still remembered by some as having realised for them . . . the secrets and the consolations of the worship of the Church.[6]

Ollard maintained, however, that the 'first step in the further revival of ceremonial was due to one whose name figures not at all in the general literature of the Movement'. This was J. R. Bloxham, a Fellow of Magdalen College until he accepted a parish in 1863 where he ministered for almost 30 years.[7] Bloxham started with an antiquarian interest in church ornament and ritual. The views of men such as Bloxham and Oakeley were not those of the founding Tractarians. For example, Keble, Pusey and the Anglican Newman feared that more elaborate ceremonial might hinder the acceptance of catholic doctrine. The picture is not entirely clear, however, because as early as 1839 Newman said, in a letter to Manning, 'give us more services, more vestments and decorations in worship'.[8]

When a new direction did emerge, the initiative came from Cambridge, not from Oxford. As an undergraduate, John Mason Neale had developed a consuming interest in church architecture and ecclesiastical practices and, with a few friends, established the Cambridge Camden Society. The origins of this Society can be traced back as far as 1839, but it became the Ecclesiological Society several years later. At first its members were interested in 'taking' or assessing the architectural merits of church buildings. Soon, though, they were making pronouncements about acceptable forms of design, and did much to promote 'Victorian gothic' as an architectural ideal.

Although Neale spent little time as a parish priest, he had a deep sense of the need to encourage people to worship. Consequently he took his ideas further than did men such as Bloxham and Oakeley. With his friends Neale wanted to draw people to worship in an environment in which symbolism could help them mature into the catholic faith. In this approach they were very different from the Tractarians who sought to establish the theological and intellectual credentials of catholic doctrine within the Church of England, and by that route bring people to worship. The two approaches were complementary and not mutually exclusive. It was the combination of them that eventually led to full-blown Anglo-Catholicism. Men such as Neale were interested in what later became known as the 'English use', but ritualism inevitably drew opponents who felt that it was merely the imitation of Roman Catholic practices and amounted to a capitulation to that Church. Gradually the opponents of ceremonial innovation became more vociferous and their activities became extreme.

It has already been noticed that Frederick Oakeley was probably the first Anglican priest to adopt a form of ceremonial that could be described as 'advanced'. Within a few years of Oakeley's secession to Rome the use of candles on the altar, for devotional purposes not for illumination, and the introduction of eucharistic vestments had begun, but were largely unremarked at first. It was argued by enthusiasts that vestments were not only legal but actually required by the rubric in the Book of Common Prayer which asserted that the attire of the minister should be that which was worn during the 'second year' of the reign of King Edward VI. There was constant argument about the precise meaning of the phrase, which was not as unequivocal as it seemed.

It was not until the 1860s that ritualistic innovations began to be noticed by the public at large, and from then the already hostile press had a new target. Ritualism seemed to be a phenomenon associated with the new generation of younger clergy. Dean Church's biographer recorded W. J. Copeland's view that some of the younger men thought his generation rather backward because of their failure, in terms of ritual, to 'do proper things'.[9] The *Edinburgh Review* in 1867 thought that liturgical innovations were something that had happened suddenly and recently, over the previous three years. This was years after the redoubtable Golightly had complained of the ceremonial used in the chapel of Cuddesdon Theological College. So great was the hubbub that Bishop Samuel Wilberforce of Oxford, who had founded the College across the road from his palace, was obliged to accept the resignation of the Vice-Principal, H. P. Liddon, who was responsible for what had gone on. To later eyes, the elaboration of ritual of which Liddon was guilty was inconsequential, but the situation was sensitive in 1859. A friend said afterwards that Liddon at Cuddesdon had been guilty of 'little ritualistic frivolities'.

By chance Liddon was asked to be the first incumbent of St Alban's, Holborn, a church built in 1863 through the generosity of the Anglo-Catholic layman and Member of Parliament, J. G. Hubbard. He declined the invitation but recommended A. H. Mackonochie. He was a man whom Liddon had got to know when they served together briefly as curates at Wantage, where their vicar was W. J. Butler who was also to be famous as a ritualist. Mackonochie was an energetic and hard-working man who made the church notorious as a ritualistic haven and remained its vicar throughout the ritualistic controversies. Eventually he died in a Scottish snowstorm whilst on holiday. Mackonochie faced eastwards to celebrate the Holy Communion, he introduced vestments in his church and also had candles on the altar. Candles were not unknown, having been used on the holy table all though the eighteenth century in many places. What was innovative was lighting them as devotional aids and not merely to provide the celebrant with light. G. R. Prynne became incumbent of St Peter's, Plymouth in 1848 which was in the diocese of Bishop Phillpotts. Prynne benefited from his bishop's protection and became famous as a very 'advanced' ritualist. He also generated controversy by publishing a *Eucharistic Manual* which argued for candles, vestments, incense and a cross either on the altar or above it. Prynne wore eucharistic vestments and burned incense in his church. Both men referred to the table on which they celebrated the eucharist as the 'altar'. This was a term that was not ruled out in the Church of England after the Reformation, but its use by such individuals was a sign of their churchmanship.

In 1865 the opponents of ritualism founded the Church Association and it was soon active in seeking to prosecute clergy. Two of the cases were particularly notable. First, Mackonochie was brought before the Court of Arches by an agent who acted for the Association. The case against Mackonochie concerned the now customary objections to the use of incense, candles on the altar, the mixing of water and wine in the chalice and the elevation of the sacred elements at the consecration. The case was heard by the Dean of Arches, now Sir Robert Phillimore, who gave a tolerant judgement which reflected old-fashioned High Churchmanship. On an appeal by the Church Association, Mackonochie was aggrieved when, as he perceived it, unfair costs were awarded against him and he was suspended from his benefice for three months. Gradually he reintroduced the practices against which Phillimore had issued his judgement.

The second notable case was the work of the Brighton branch of the Church Association which was particularly active and attacked J. M. Neale at East Grinstead. The Association also turned its attention to John Purchas of St James', Brighton. He had faced complaints about his ritual innovations within months of his appointment in 1866, one of which was a stuffed dove suspended above the altar at Pentecost. The church had been of an evangelical persuasion before his appointment, so it is likely that passions were at a high level. Once again Phillimore tried to be fair, although Purchas had refused to appear when the case was heard.[10] Purchas had the support of an Anglo-Catholic society, the English Church Union, but it refused to support his more extravagant practices and was cautiously happy with Phillimore's ruling. The Church Association was not at all happy and took the case to the Judicial Committee of the Privy Council which overturned most of what Phillimore had said was permissible. A petition of clergy gained 4,700 signatures but failed to get a new hearing, but the new Bishop of Chichester, Richard Durnford, refused to enforce the suspension of Purchas. For his part, in order to avoid the crippling costs such as Mackonochie had faced, Purchas transferred his property to his wife. The case was still unresolved when Purchas died in 1872. These two cases serve to illustrate the limitations of the system of clerical discipline. The only sanctions which the bishops and the law could impose were suspension, and the award of costs against the defendant. The issuing of directives whether episcopal or legal was ineffective, as the clergy knew that they could disregard them with impunity.

A. C. Tait, no friend of the Anglo-Catholics and similarly hostile to ritual embellishment of church services, became Archbishop of Canterbury in 1868. He was translated from London where he had encountered ritualistic clergy such as Mackonochie. Within a couple of years of Tait's appointment, despite the failure of the *Edinburgh Review* to have noticed, the number of ritualistic parishes had grown to the extent that opponents were beginning to demand action against the offending clergy. It has been estimated that by 1870 there were 442 parish clergy of incumbent status who could be described as Tractarian.[11] Only a minority of them could be regarded as thoroughgoing ritualists, but most would have employed some degree of ceremonial to promote their teaching. Generally speaking, ritualist clergy were to be found in towns, and mostly in the southern half of the country. Yates has recently questioned this generalization, but acknowledged that the largest number of ritualist churches were to be found in the greater London area.

An important incumbent in London was W. J. E. Bennett who, as early as 1851, endured riots and civil disturbance from crowds who sought to break up services held in another newly-built Anglo-Catholic shrine, the parish church of St Barnabas, Pimlico. Another London priest, Bryan King, suffered in a similar manner in 1859–60, because of the ritualistic practices which he introduced in his parish of St George's in the East. Both men had used eucharistic vestments, lighted candles and had faced eastwards at the altar. A similar liturgical regime was in force at St Peter's, London Docks, under the care of C. F. Lowder, and caused anxiety for Tait as Bishop of London. At first he turned a blind eye, but when he received a formal complaint he issued instructions. Lowder took little notice of his diocesan bishop, and in this was typical of many ritualistic clergy. Their indifference arose from the fact that many of them were socially well connected, accustomed to having their own way and not the sort of men to be browbeaten by a bishop or anyone else. It was also clear that the episcopate was almost helpless in the face of their intransigence because of the lack of enforceable sanctions.

Lord Shaftesbury, Pusey's fiercely evangelical relative, tried to introduce anti-ritualistic legislation in the late 1860s, but had not succeeded in his attempts. However, a Royal Commission was set up in 1867 to look into the question of ritual. The Commission failed to produce a report with any degree of unanimity and, as a result, the government did not feel able to pursue the matter of regulating ritual. But the contentious atmosphere did not abate and eventually Tait decided that the situation must be addressed. Many years before, Keble, who had died in 1866, had expressed horror at the 'suicidal' prospect of 'lovers of the Church . . . opening the door to Parliamentary interference with spiritual matters',[12] but this was exactly what Tait planned. His opportunity came in 1874 when the Tories, under Disraeli, won the general election. Everyone had expected Gladstone to win, and Disraeli had not even devised a legislative programme. Tait had approached Gladstone before the election, and had received a reply counselling caution. Tait, who would have thought Keble's anxiety unfounded, disregarded Gladstone's advice, and took advantage of the situation. Disraeli's espousal of the cause, which he called 'a Bill to put down ritualism', brought to an end the traditional identification of the Tractarians with the Tory party. It was a significantly erastian proposal, and some opposed it for that reason. Christopher Wordsworth, Bishop of Lincoln from 1868, worked against the Bill because he was convinced that it would drive clergy to Rome and it made the Church of England appear to be completely subject to the state.[13]

With the support of Archbishop Thomson of York, Tait suggested that Parliament should pass a Bill regulating the conduct of church services. The Bill which became the Public Worship Regulation Act was introduced in the House of Lords by Archbishop Tait. He had previously told the bishops that such an Act was desired by the Queen, and she was known to distrust the Tractarians and to detest ritualists. Tait had been reluctant to consult Convocation about the Bill, as some of the bishops desired. He felt, with some justification, that it would not meet with the approval of the Lower House. This added to the perception that he was acting in a high-handed manner. This was compounded when he allowed his proposals to be leaked to *The Times*, which provoked a reaction from a number of clergy.

Pusey alleged that few clergy were breaking the law. Predictably he observed that Parliament, which included among its members Roman Catholics, Dissenters and non-believers, was not a suitable body to legislate on the discipline of the clergy of the Church of England. His response to Tait was published as a pamphlet. Pusey's intervention was inevitably at the intellectual level. Others reacted differently. When the likelihood that the Act would indeed become law dawned upon the ritualists, it was hardly surprising that their attitude hardened. The Bill was controversial and had a stormy passage; not least it suffered a fierce attack in the House of Commons from Gladstone, who wanted the whole thing scrapped. When it was passed, the Queen personally congratulated Disraeli and wrote in a similar vein to Tait.

The stage was now set to make the ritualists answerable before the law of the land. In the sense that it was a hastily contrived piece of legislation, the Public Worship Regulation Act was similar to the Ecclesiastical Titles Act which had attempted to control the establishment of the Roman Catholic hierarchy. The new Act gave the bishops the right to veto any proposed prosecution, and this proved to be its saving grace. What it had not considered was the nature of the sanction or punishment which would be handed down to recalcitrant clergy under its provisions, but no one knew that this oversight would cause problems. The Act allowed appeals to the Judicial Committee of the Privy Council, which was already known to be unacceptable to High Churchmen. But before the new court could hear any cases, it required the appointment of a layman as judge, and Lord Penzance was chosen. He was not an ecclesiastical lawyer, and had built his reputation in the divorce court. High Churchmen were horrified by the appointment.

In the country at large there was considerable support for the new Act.[14] Many thought that it would indeed 'put down ritualism'. It caused a few secessions to Rome; other clergy quietly complied and reverted to their former practices. Others decided to fight, adopting Mackonochie's motto, 'no surrender, no desertion'. Manning, who had followed Wiseman as Cardinal Archbishop of Westminster, had called ritualism the exercise of 'private judgement in gorgeous raiment', but a common mind was gradually being reached. This took final shape in the year after the passage of the Act, when the English Church Union, one of many Anglo-Catholic societies but arguably the most important, proposed its 'six points'. These defined the most important ritualistic practices. They were the use of vestments; the eastward position of the celebrant at the altar; candles or altar lights; the mixture of water and wine in the chalice; the use of wafer bread and also the use of incense. Tait and Disraeli had reckoned without the Anglo-Catholics' conviction that matters of principle were at stake. As J. S. Reed observed, 'by the 1870s the objectives of [the Act] were perhaps unattainable in any case, but this legislation was especially ill-designed for its purpose'.[15] Seventeen clergy were attacked by the Church Association within four years of the Act being passed. Five of the cases were not resolved without recourse to the new court.

The first case that of the Reverend C. J. Ridsdale of St Peter's, Folkestone, in Tait's own diocese. The grounds for this prosecution were similar to those already described, as were the other prosecutions under the Act. Ridsdale declared that his appearance before Lord Penzance should not be taken as his acceptance of the court's spiritual jurisdiction. As we have seen, it was quite usual for ritualists to refuse to acknowledge the authority of the court, but when Penzance ruled against him, Ridsdale took the step of appealing to the Judicial Committee of the Privy Council concerning the legality of the use of vestments, wafer bread and the eastward position at the altar. He also appealed for the use of candles and for a crucifix on the rood screen. The Committee ruled against him. Ridsdale, who had recently married and understandably did not want to jeopardize his home and livelihood, eventually accepted the decision and made his peace with Tait.

The case of a second priest occurred before the resolution of the Ridsdale case. The accused clergyman was Arthur Tooth, the incumbent of St James's church, Hatcham, which was in the Diocese of Rochester. He refused to obey Lord Penzance's injunction to give up certain of his ritualistic practices, nor would he accept suspension from his benefice. He claimed that, whatever the legal position, his suspension was 'spiritually null and void'. The Bishop of Rochester sent other clergy to take services in the parish, but Tooth and his supporters locked them out and there were scenes of considerable disorder. Much was made in the press of the riots at Hatcham and elsewhere but, although there were deplorable scenes, they did not affect the outcome of the situation. He was eventually sent to prison, in January 1877, for contempt of court, which he refused to purge in order to obtain his release. He was in Horsemonger Gaol for 28 days and a satirist described him as 'The Tooth that will not come out.' On his release, which (remarkably) was sought by his opponents, he was hailed as a Tractarian hero and martyr.

Next came the case of Thomas Pelham Dale, of St Vedast's, Foster Lane, in the City of London. The Bishop of London had unsuccessfully tried to prosecute him in 1877, but the Church Association was more successful. Dale was gaoled in October 1880, but Tait criticized the Association for its action. Once again the charges followed the now familiar pattern, and Dale spent 49 days in prison and was released after a resort to a *habeas corpus*. It was already becoming apparent that the Public Worship Regulation Act was causing embarrassment and failing to solve any problems. Privately, and with the tacit approval of Archbishop Tait, diocesan bishops began to negotiate with ritualistic clergy. R. W. Church, the Dean of St Paul's from 1871, disapproved of negotiations. He felt that the matters in dispute should be addressed. He also witnessed an attempt by two residentiary canons, Liddon and Robert Gregory, to get the Bishop of London to prosecute them in order to 'draw the fire' away from parish clergy. Bishop Jackson wisely declined to enter the lists with two such prominent and able clergy. A later Bishop of London, Frederick Temple, exercised his episcopal veto when an attempt was made to prosecute the Dean and Chapter of St Paul's for installing a reredos with statues of the Blessed Virgin and other saints.

Fourth in the list of clergy who suffered under the Act was R. W. Enraght, vicar of Holy Trinity, Bordesley. He was condemned by Penzance on no less than 16 points of ritual and found himself in Warwick Gaol from November 1880 until the following January. He was the third man to go to prison. On his release he continued his ritualistic practices for a further two years.

Another parish clergyman to be prosecuted under the Act was the vicar of St John's, Miles Platting in the Diocese of Manchester, S. F. Green. The charitable and capable Bishop of Manchester, James Fraser, had previously tried to moderate Green's ritualistic practices to no effect. Once again it was the Church Association which tried to tackle him. Again it was the usual list of offences. Fraser was asked to exercise his episcopal veto, but it was left too late. Penzance issued an inhibition which Green ignored. In November 1880, he was found guilty of contempt of court and taken to Lancaster Gaol in March 1881. Green remained in prison until November 1882 and has the unenviable distinction of serving the longest of all the ritualistic 'martyrs'. When he came out, his living had been declared vacant under the terms of the Public Worship Regulation Act.

The last priest to suffer imprisonment was James Bell Cox, the vicar of St Margaret's, Toxteth Park. His parish was in the Diocese of Liverpool whose bishop was J. C. Ryle, a notable opponent of ritualism. Bell Cox was in Walton Gaol for just over a fortnight in May 1887. By this time there had developed a general dislike of the effects of the Act. People were unhappy to see conscientious clergy put in prison for offences that many regarded as inconsequential. Public opinion did not like ritualism, but felt it was misguided rather than criminal. Even some of the vociferous evangelical newspapers, such as *The Record*, abandoned their enthusiasm for litigation. The fact that the imprisonments were for contempt of court was largely disregarded.

After these prosecutions, no more priests were committed to prison and, following the Green case, the practice of prosecutions ceased – with one exception. The Church Association made one last attempt to put an end to ritualism by prosecuting the Bishop of Lincoln. Edward King had been consecrated to the Diocese in 1885 following the death of Bishop Wordsworth, and was recognized as a man of great holiness of life. He was also a committed Anglo-Catholic and is thought to be the first Anglican bishop since the Reformation to wear a mitre. King had been appointed to Lincoln at the instigation of Gladstone who, as Prime Minister, tried to follow a balanced policy of episcopal appointments in terms of churchmanship. King was denounced for ritual offences committed in a parish church in Lincoln, and also in his cathedral. The importance of the case was, of course, due to the position occupied by the defendant. After some deliberation, Archbishop Edward Benson decided to hear the case himself in Lambeth Palace, assisted by a number of fellow bishops who were described as 'assessors'. The learned Bishop Stubbs was one of five episcopal assessors whom Benson appointed to assist him. A remark made by Stubbs was often quoted: 'this is not a court, it is an Archbishop sitting in his library'. Liddon referred to some of the unofficial spectators as 'great ecclesiastical ladies'. Benson asked King to make some minor concessions in his practice, and the Church Association was so dissatisfied that it took the matter to the Judicial Committee of the Privy Council which upheld Benson's decision. Far from achieving its aims, the Church Association was left with a new situation in which the Lincoln case became the touchstone by which ritual practices were judged.

The question of ritual has taken the story of the Oxford Movement forward, and it is now necessary to consider the matter of auricular or sacramental confession which, although obviously linked to the matter of ritual observances, is a distinct element of life for a catholic Christian. The Anglican case for an individual to make his or her confession can be made by reference to the Book of Common Prayer, particularly a rubric in the order for the Visitation of the Sick. There is also a reference to such a ministry in the first Exhortation in the Prayer Book service of Holy Communion. Reed, in *Glorious Battle*, noticed that the practice was not unknown to the old-fashioned High Churchmen. An interesting example of the old approach is seen in the teaching of W. F. Hook. In his parish in Leeds he encouraged auricular confession at times 'of great spiritual emergencies'[16] and, in accordance with the Book of Common Prayer, at times of illness. It was, however, comparatively rare, but not unknown.

Pusey was the instigator of the revival of the practice in the Church of England, having advocated the use of sacramental confession as early as 1838. 'Consciences are burdened', he wrote. 'There is provision, on the part of God, in His Church, to relieve them.'[17] He advocated confession, not merely for troubled consciences, but also as an appropriate preparation for receiving Holy Communion. In 1846 he preached an explicit sermon on confession at the end of his suspension, and published it with the title, *The Entire Absolution of the Penitent*. In 1873 he was behind a carefully drafted 'Declaration' sent to Convocation in protest against a scheme to license confessors. Keble was also a devotee of the sacrament of auricular confession. He saw the practice as a pastoral tool by which a clergyman could help his parishioners to live in a holy and devout manner. When advocating confession, he referred to an exhortation which can be found in the 1549 Prayer Book. As early as 1826 Hurrell Froude had used Keble as his confessor. Like Keble, Pusey was to gain much experience of hearing confessions, and they both experienced direct and spontaneous approaches from individuals. Pusey and Keble had not been enamoured of ritualism, so their commitment to the practice of auricular confession is an important link between the surviving Tractarians and their Anglo-Catholic followers. In the early days of the Oxford Movement, Tractarian clergy tended to use their friends as their confessors. When Bishop Wilberforce required Liddon, on his appointment as Vice-Principal of his newly founded Theological College at Cuddesdon in 1854, to change from Pusey to Keble as his confessor, the former graciously said that he 'was giving up brass for gold'.

Anglican clergy, by and large, did not know how to help people with their confession, and it is remarkable that there were few scandals as a result of inexperience. One anxiety was that the Tractarians tended to place too great an emphasis on penance and this was sometimes unhealthy. Certainly, there was a morbid streak in Pusey's personality which some thought laid him open to this fault. As the practice spread the Anglo-Catholics took very seriously the need for training. One of the High-Church organizations, the Society of the Holy Cross, had been behind a petition to Convocation as late as 1873 which asked for the selection, training and licensing of suitable clergy for this ministry. Whilst it was clear that clergy could and should be helped to become skilful confessors, the idea of a specific authorization process by Convocation was abhorrent to Pusey and his friends, for authorization is clearly given in the Ordinal.

As soon as the advocacy of confession became known, it was immediately controversial. Blomfield and Tait, successive Bishops of London, resisted it. The latter disciplined a curate, by withdrawing his licence, for advocating it. There were three main reasons why the revival of auricular confession excited fierce enmity.

The first was the familiar fear of what stout Protestants called 'popery', although Charles Marriott believed that the unavailability of sacramental confession within the Church of England had been a cause of secessions.[18] Confession was feared as yet another romanizing practice, a novelty which was alien to the Church of England. Associated with this visceral fear of the Church of Rome was a feeling that for a person to make his or her confession was somehow to behave in a manner that was 'unEnglish'.

The second objection touched Victorian sensibilities. Confession was seen as an encroachment on family life. Many of the publications opposing the practice expressed profound horror and disquiet about learning the secrets of families. A good example of the near hysteria is the following, which was written by Canon Stowell of Salford:

> I will suppress my own feelings though they are ready to boil over; and I will not stir up the feelings of others, though I am sure the honest feelings of every Englishman, of every father, of every brother, of every husband, are startled when he thinks of the sister, the wife, the daughter, or the mother going into the dark den of the confessional.[19]

Archbishop Thomson of York did not want exposed 'the sacredness of the hearth to a prying and often morbid curiosity'.[20] Another protagonist thought that hearing confessions should be a capital offence! The language was so strong that one is left with the feeling that the objectors feared that there was much in Victorian family life that should not be exposed to scrutiny.

This links with the third reason why the practice excited such opposition. In order to be effective, a confessor might need to elicit information from the penitent. This led the enemies of the practice to fear what one called 'filthy interrogations'. The great emphasis that was put on this side of things led Mackonochie to observe that the opponents thought that confessors neglected nine of the Ten Commandments. George Prynne found himself in difficulties over the hearing of confessions. Prynne had become Vicar of St Peter's, Plymouth in 1848. He was a convinced ritualist and was happy to be associated with Miss Sellon and her sisterhood. From the first he was an advocate of the practice of hearing confessions, and soon realized that the moral climate in the naval town of Plymouth needed to be addressed in his dealings with female penitents. In 1852 he added to his controversial reputation when he published a pamphlet stoutly defending confession. More publicity came when it was revealed in the press that he sometimes felt it necessary in the confessional to ask penitents leading questions regarding 'purity'. When attacked he defended himself to Bishop Phillpotts in a lengthy letter. In it he spelled out and justified his practice. He wrote:

> Those who are in the habit of receiving confessions know that persons often have deep and painful sins to confess which they have a difficulty or a delicacy in expressing, and if the confessor were not to help such persons by kind and judicious questions they . . . would go away only half relieved, and we could not in that case honestly grant them absolution 'from all their sins'.

Another reason by which Prynne justified his approach was that 'a confessor will often see that persons have no idea how gravely they have offended till he has brought it home to them by searching questions'.[21] Phillpotts experienced mob violence when conducting a confirmation at St Peter's, but he stuck by Prynne and commended his conscientiousness. Much of the fear was generated because it was thought that the majority of penitents were women. C. F. Lowder agreed that this was likely to be so, on the grounds that women had always been more devout. He went on to say that the hearing of confessions was not a task that any priest would lightly undertake. Bishop Wilberforce reminded people that confession was 'medicine not food'.

Although the matter of sacramental confession was part of the priestly ministry of Keble and Pusey, the ambivalence towards ritualism in their minds must be addressed in the debate as to whether it was ever properly part of the Oxford Movement. There are, however, two important issues which must be considered in conclusion. The first is the question as to whether the principles of the Tractarians would have survived if they had not eventually been expressed through the enhancement of worship. Without ritualism it is possible that, like other essentially intellectual movements, it would have faded away. Second, as a result of the other elements of Victorian taste, church services might have undergone development and elaboration even if the Tractarian phenomenon had not occurred. Had that been the case, ritualism would have lacked a theological root, and would have been no more than a passing fashion. This would have been part of what Gladstone meant by his telling phrase, 'high ritual with a low appreciation of Christian doctrine'.[22]

Tractarianism provided the intellectual and theological rationale which was essential if ritualism were to become part of the life of the Church of England in the nineteenth century. It was a combination of these factors that created such a volatile situation in the Church towards the end of the century. Supporters and opponents of the Oxford Movement found that their deepest convictions clashed. Progress could only be made by way of controversies and setbacks. Eventually a synthesis was achieved and the verdict of history must be that the Oxford Movement made a unique and permanent contribution to the self-understanding of the Church of England and, in due course, to the whole Anglican Communion.

Chapter 8

Last Words

As the means of assessing the success of a movement, the funerals of the chief men might be considered unusual, but it is not inappropriate. John Keble died at Bournemouth in the early hours of 29 March 1866, six weeks before his wife and a month short of his 74th birthday. He had never attracted the odium which Pusey's name drew. He had, however, been clearly identified with the Oxford Movement from the beginning, although there was much about him of the Tory High Churchman of earlier generations. Newman, as is well known, dated the whole enterprise from July 1833 when John Keble preached the Assize Sermon in St Mary's church. Newman was guilty of an over-simplification, but had readily acknowledged that Keble was in the thick of events from the start. Keble's devotional poetry, particularly *The Christian Year*, was immensely popular and had made him a household name before 1833. The references to his piety and self-effacing goodness are too numerous and well-attested to be other than genuine, but he had been a doughty fighter with that element of intolerance and single-mindedness which is necessary for a partisan. Indeed, J. A. Froude, who had learned to despise Tractarianism, said of him, 'if he had not been Keble he would have been called (treason though it be to write the words) narrow minded'.[1] These character-istics together with his contributions to the *Tracts for the Times*, and his willing involvement in the events which they provoked, meant that he could not avoid being a controversial figure.

Hursley church and churchyard were crowded for his funeral, which serves to illustrate that his opinions and principles had achieved a wide appeal by the time of his death. Nearly 80 people attended the early morning communion service and the funeral itself saw an overcrowded church. It was, as a modern biographer described the scene, a 'sea of black . . . and half the world seemed to be gathered there in mourning'.[2] The Deans of St Paul's and of Chichester, R. W. Church and W. F. Hook, 'were glad to get a school children's bench in a corner'.[3] Church noticed that there were many younger clergy among those present, and supposed a little ruefully and not entirely with approval, that Keble belonged to the new generation as much as he did to the old. The notion of a new college to be built in Oxford as his memorial was aired by Liddon privately after the funeral. Fund-raising started almost at once and Keble College became a reality within a few years. Such a memorial bears witness to the esteem in which the man and his views were held.

A few months later John Mason Neale, one of the younger generation and an Anglo-Catholic firebrand, died at the comparatively early age of 48. Once again the funeral was a triumph. Neale had crowded much into his comparatively short life. A completely uncompromising High Churchman and ritualist, he had founded the sisterhood of St Margaret. He also had won fame as a prolific writer whose best efforts were genuinely of a high intellectual calibre, but who was also skilful as a populist although his novels have not endured. He wrote extensively on hymnody, had produced the first English history of Eastern Christianity and a large commentary on the Psalms. He had composed many hymns of his own and translated a large number of Greek and Latin hymns from antiquity. He had been forced to exercise a circumscribed ministry as Warden of some East Grinstead almshouses. Throughout it all, he had been a champion of Anglo-Catholicism who had won a real degree of notoriety. His funeral took place in the parish church, from which he had once been banned for his catholic practices. The procession of clergy, of laity, of the sisterhood and of many others, made a spectacular procession which crowded the streets. Local people literally climbed to roof-tops to view it passing to the church. The sisterhood which Neale had founded had already spread into many fields of work. Such communities extended the influence of the Oxford Movement and enabled devout women to exercise a ministry of prayer and of service to the community.

Pusey survived them all. He had been almost overcome with grief at the death of Keble, but lived on until September 1882. He was 82 when he died at Ascot Priory. He was buried in Christ Church Cathedral next to his wife, their daughter Lucy and another who had died in infancy. Pusey had been the Oxford Movement's fixed point in the difficult years after the secession of Newman and the hard times which followed. He had been the subject of 'profound disappointments . . . of unchecked obloquy and wanton insult', said Dean Church later, but he had also been the recipient of 'boundless reverence and trust'.[4] It was as an elder statesman that he was regarded by many at the time of his death. Once again this was demonstrated at the funeral. It was attended by very large numbers of people, 'the procession of clergy, five or six abreast, reached round three sides of the Great Quadrangle'.[5] and the cathedral was full of mourners. One of the mourners was the Prime Minister, W. E. Gladstone. Among the hymns sung was Newman's 'Lead kindly light'. Pusey had expressed disquiet at the opinions of some of the younger disciples of the Tractarian movement, and had never been completely reconciled to the activities of the more advanced ritualists. All, however, revered him as a warrior and a prophet who had made an immense contribution to the Church of God.

Liddon once again took the lead in securing a permanent memorial to Pusey. Money was raised for the purchase of his library and some appropriate premises in which to accommodate it. Pusey House in Oxford was the eventual outcome. Again, it was a memorial which demonstrated the greatness of the man. In 1870, H. P. Liddon, the disciple and confidant of Pusey, was appointed to a Residentiary Canonry at St Paul's Cathedral, and almost simultaneously elected to an Oxford professorship. He had made his academic reputation with the Bampton Lectures of 1866 which ran to 14 published editions and were translated into German. Always a conservative scholar, Liddon was already famous as a preacher by the time he went to St Paul's, and for 20 years he drew enormous congregations to hear his sermons. People queued for over an hour to get a place under the crowded dome, and then listened for even longer. His sermons, which were subsequently published, were unashamedly catholic in their presentation of theological truth, and he made no concessions with the doctrinal content of his lengthy discourses. With his two appointments, Liddon exercised an influential ministry among future clergy at Oxford and among large numbers of lay people at St Paul's. Liddon was distressed at the direction taken by some of the work of Charles Gore, the first Librarian of Pusey House. In 1889 he edited a series of essays with the title *Lux Mundi*. This, in the words of Gore's preface, 'attempted to put the Catholic faith into its right relation to modern intellectual and moral problems'.[6] *Lux Mundi* was a remarkable piece of work undertaken by 11 scholars with Anglo-Catholic sympathies and marked the way in which the successors of the Tractarians helped to prepare the Anglican Church to face the challenges of the twentieth century and beyond.

Gradually clergy with catholic principles began to be represented in the higher levels of the Church of England. Some of them have been noticed in these pages, but it was an uphill struggle. Queen Victoria regarded Anglo-Catholics as dangerous enemies within the Church of England and so, partly because of her views, there was not a great deal of preferment given to them. This factor makes the emergence of men such as Richard Church and Liddon particularly noticeable in the early 1870s. High Churchmen with some sympathy for Tractarianism received preferment as the century wore on. One such was W. F. Hook, a notable parish clergyman with a lengthy ministry in Coventry and then in Leeds. He was made Dean of Chichester in 1859. Bishop Samuel Wilberforce of Oxford, who had tolerated the ardent Anglo-Catholicism of Liddon as Vice-Principal of Cuddesdon Theological College, was translated to Winchester in 1869 and the influence of the Oxford Movement gradually spread. Charles Gore was successively Bishop of Worcester, Birmingham and Oxford. Francis Paget and E. S. Talbot were among the *Lux Mundi* scholars and both also became diocesan bishops. Henry Scott Holland became a Canon of St Paul's and a Regius Professor at Oxford.

By far the greatest expression of the life of the Church of England is to be found in its parishes, and no movement could succeed unless it made a very significant impact among parishioners. Gradually this came about as increasing numbers of the clergy came to reflect, in varying degrees, the teaching which underpinned the whole message of the Oxford Movement. There is no precise way to measure the spread of this influence, and any attempt to do so inevitably looks at the more easily assessed phenomenon of ritualism. By 1881, J. A. Froude, the younger brother of Hurrell, had become a severe and implacable enemy of the Oxford Movement. Even so, he was forced ruefully to admit, 'there is scarcely a clergyman in the country who does not carry upon him in one form or another the marks of the Tractarian movement'.[7] A more friendly commentator was S. L. Ollard, writing in 1915, who took the matter beyond the clergy and referred to the 'memorial which every parish in England now bears to him'. He was speaking of Keble, but his phrase 'every parish' is an oblique reference to all who had worked to establish Tractarian principles. Elsewhere the same author wrote of 'the working men and women whose lives are lighted and whose work is dignified by that faith . . . which has come to them through the prayers and labours of the men of the Oxford Movement'.[8]

Notes

1 Origins of the Oxford Movement

1 R. W. Church, *The Oxford Movement: Twelve Years 1833–1845* (London, Macmillan, 1891), p. 1.
2 W. E. Gladstone, 'Ritual and Ritualism', *Contemporary Review* No. 24 (1874), p. 669.
3 J. H. Newman, *Tract 90*, p. 6. References are to the 1841 edn, repr. with a historical commentary by A. W. Evans (London, Constable, 1933).
4 O. Chadwick, *The Victorian Church*, 1 (London, A. & C. Black, 1966), p. 9.
5 W. Palmer, *A Narrative of Events connected with the publication of the Tracts for the Times* (enlarged edn, London, Rivingtons, 1883), p. 96. References to 'William Palmer of Worcester College' distinguish him from a namesake who was a Fellow of Magdalen College.
6 Palmer, *A Narrative of Events*, p. 96.
7 Y. Brilioth, *The Anglican Revival: Studies in the Oxford Movement* (London, Longmans, Green, 1933), p. 14.
8 Church, *The Oxford Movement*, p. 3.
9 P. B. Nockles, *The Oxford Movement in Context: Anglican High Churchmanship 1760–1857* (Cambridge, Cambridge University Press, 1994).
10 Church, *The Oxford Movement*, p. 10.
11 Church, *The Oxford Movement*, pp. 3–4.
12 J. H. Newman, *Apologia pro vita sua* (1864) p. 57. References are to the Penguin Books edn, 1994.
13 Chadwick, *The Victorian Church*, 1, p. 53.

14 Newman, *Apologia*, p. 31.
15 A. P. Stanley, *The Life and Correspondence of Thomas Arnold, D.D.* (London, John Murray, 1892), p. 191.
16 Quoted in Chadwick, *The Victorian Church*, 1, p. 47.
17 Newman, *Apologia*, pp. 47–8.
18 Newman, *Apologia*, p. 46.
19 Newman, *Apologia*, p. 46.
20 Newman, *Apologia*, p. 47.
21 Newman, *Apologia*, p. 48.
22 Newman, *Apologia*, p. 50.
23 Newman, *Apologia*, p. 50.
24 J. A. Froude, *Short Studies on Great Subjects* (London, Longmans, Green, 1894), 4, p. 264.
25 G. Battiscombe, *John Keble: A Study in Limitations* (London, Constable, 1963), p. 118.
26 I. Ker, *John Henry Newman: A Biography* (Oxford, Oxford University Press, 1988), pp. 116, 121.
27 Church, *The Oxford Movement*, pp. 24, 25.
28 Chadwick, *The Victorian Church*, 1, p. 68.

2 Early Progress

 1 J. T. Coleridge, *A Memoir of the Reverend John Keble, M.A.* (Oxford, Parker, 1870), p. 221.
 2 Coleridge, *A Memoir*, p. 218.
 3 John Keble, 'National Apostasy', Assize Sermon, p. 13. All references are to the centenary Commemorative Edition (Steventon, Rocket Press, 1983).
 4 Keble, Assize Sermon, p. 11, preface to the first edn.
 5 Keble, Assize Sermon, pp. 14–15.
 6 Keble, Assize Sermon, p. 16.
 7 Keble, Assize Sermon, p. 17.
 8 Keble, Assize Sermon, p. 18.
 9 Keble, Assize Sermon, p. 20.
10 Keble, Assize Sermon, p. 16.
11 Keble, Assize Sermon, p. 21.
12 O. Chadwick, *The Victorian Church*, 1 (London, A. & C. Black, 1966), p. 71.
13 T. Mozley, *Reminiscences chiefly of Oriel College and the Oxford Movement* (London, Longmans, Green, 1882), 1, p. 308.

14 R. W. Church, *The Oxford Movement: Twelve Years 1833–1845* (London, Macmillan, 1891), p. 97.

15 H. P. Liddon, *The Life of E. B. Pusey, D.D.* (London, Longmans, Green, 1893–7), 1, p. 267.

16 S. L. Ollard, *A Short History of the Oxford Movement* (London, Mowbray, 1915, repr. 1983), p. 29.

17 Church, *The Oxford Movement*, p. 98.

18 W. Palmer, *A Narrative of Events connected with the publication of the Tracts for the Times* (Oxford, J. H. Parker, 1843; enlarged with an Introduction and Supplement, London, Rivingtons, 1883), p. 102.

19 Church, *The Oxford Movement*, p. 105.

20 Palmer, *Narrative of Events*, p. 105.

21 A. P. Perceval, *A Collection of Papers connected with the Theological Movement of 1833* (London, Rivington, etc., 1842), p. 18.

22 Liddon, *Life of Pusey*, 1, p. 277.

23 Liddon, *Life of Pusey*, 1, pp. 271–2.

24 W. J. Conybeare, *Edinburgh Review* 200 (October 1853), p. 323.

25 J. H. Newman, *Apologia pro vita sua* (1846; repr. London, Penguin, 1994), p. 57.

26 Newman, *Apologia*, p. 56.

27 Newman, *Apologia*, p. 69.

28 I. Ker, *John Henry Newman: A Biography* (Oxford: Oxford University Press, 1988), p. 135.

29 Mozley, *Reminiscences*, 1, p. 330.

30 Newman, *Apologia*, p. 56.

31 Church, *The Oxford Movement*, p. 110.

32 Newman, *Apologia*, p. 34.

33 G. Prevost (ed.), *The Autobiography of Isaac Williams, B.D.* (London, Longmans, Green, 1892), p. 70.

34 Newman, *Apologia*, p. 72.

35 Prevost (ed.), *Isaac Williams*, pp. 71–2.

36 Newman, *Apologia*, p. 71.

37 Liddon, *Life of Pusey*, 1, p. 280.

38 Liddon, *Life of Pusey*, 1, p. 287.

39 Newman, *Apologia*, p. 71.

40 O. Chadwick, *The Spirit of the Oxford Movement: Tractarian Essays* (Cambridge, Cambridge University Press, 1990), p. 135.

41 Ollard, *A Short History of the Oxford Movement*, p. 48.

42 Newman, *Apologia*, p. 72.

43 Liddon, *Life of Pusey*, 1, p. 282.

44 Walter Walsh, *The Secret History of the Oxford Movement* (London, C. J. Thynne, 1899).
45 Church, *The Oxford Movement*, p. 266.
46 Newman, *Apologia*, p. 154.
47 Church, *The Oxford Movement*, pp. 120–1.
48 Y. Brilioth, *The Anglican Revival: Studies in the Oxford Movement* (London, Longmans, Green, 1933), pp. 132–3.
49 Newman, *Apologia*, p. 66.

3 Controversies

1 W. Palmer, *Narrative of Events connected with the publication of the Tracts for the Times* (enlarged edn, London, Rivingtons, 1883), p. 128.
2 I. Ker, *John Henry Newman: A Biography* (Oxford, Oxford University Press, 1988), p. 136.
3 C. H. Smythe, 'Renn Dickson Hampden: Modernist (1793–1868), I', *Theology* 18 (1929), pp. 259–65, p. 261.
4 H. P. Liddon, *The Life of E. B. Pusey* (London, Longmans, Green, 1893–7), 1, p. 370.
5 Palmer, *Narrative*, p. 129.
6 Palmer, *Narrative*, p. 129.
7 Unacknowledged quotation in P. Ziegler, *Melbourne: A Biography of William Lamb, 2nd Viscount Melbourne* (London, Collins, 1976), p. 219.
8 T. Mozley, *Reminiscences chiefly of Oriel College and the Oxford Movement* (London, Longmans, Green, 1882), 1, ch. 58.
9 Liddon, *Life of Pusey*, 1, pp. 362–3.
10 Smythe, 'Renn Dickson Hampden, I', p. 265.
11 J. H. Newman, 'Elucidations of Dr Hampden's Theological Statements', p. 4, quoted by Liddon, *Life of Pusey*, 1, p. 371.
12 O. Chadwick, *The Victorian Church*, 1 (London, A. & C. Black, 1966), p. 238.
13 Liddon, *Life of Pusey*, 1, p. 376.
14 Quoted by Chadwick, *The Victorian Church*, 1, p. 119, n. 1.
15 C. H. Smythe, 'Renn Dickson Hampden: Modernist (1793–1868), II', *Theology* 18 (1929), pp. 313–22, p. 314.
16 Thomas Arnold, 'The Oxford Malignants and Dr Hampden', *Edinburgh Review* (April 1836), pp. 225–39, p. 236.
17 A. P. Stanley, *The Life and Correspondence of Thomas Arnold, D.D.* (London, Ward Lock, 1893), p. 270.

18 Arnold, 'The Oxford Malignants', p. 229.

19 Smythe, 'Renn Dickson Hampden, I', p. 265.

20 Liddon, *Life of Pusey*, 1, p. 425. Pusey's letter to Keble included a definition of the project: 'Library of Catholic Fathers of the Holy Church Universal anterior to the division of the East and West. Translated by Members of the Anglican Church, with notices of the respective Fathers, and brief notes by the Editors when required, and Indices.'

21 Liddon, *Life of Pusey*, 1, p. 425.

22 Liddon, *Life of Pusey*, 1, p. 427.

23 Liddon, *Life of Pusey*, 1, pp. 417–18.

24 Liddon, *Life of Pusey*, 1, p. 410.

25 Liddon, *Life of Pusey*, 1, p. 418.

26 Liddon, *Life of Pusey*, 1, p. 417.

27 Liddon, *Life of Pusey*, 1, pp. 445–7.

28 Mozley, *Reminiscences*, 1, p. 415.

29 Liddon, *Life of Pusey*, 1, p. 433.

30 Mozley, *Reminiscences*, 1, p. 225.

31 J. A. Froude, *Short Studies on Great Subjects* (London, Longmans, Green, 1894), 4, p. 249.

32 J. H. Newman and J. Keble (eds.), *The Remains of the late Reverend Richard Hurrell Froude* (London, Rivington, 1838), 1, p. 438.

33 J. H. Newman, *Apologia pro vita sua* (London, Penguin, 1994), p. 41.

34 G. Battiscombe, *John Keble: A Study in Limitations* (London, Constable, 1963), p. 199.

35 J. T. Coleridge, *A Memoir of the Reverend John Keble* (Oxford, Parker, 1870), p. 143.

36 Froude's *Remains*, 1, preface, p. v.

37 Froude's *Remains*, 1, preface, p. vi.

38 Froude's *Remains*, 1, p. 44.

39 Froude's *Remains*, 1, p. 28.

40 Coleridge, *A Memoir*, p. 255.

41 P. Brendon, *Hurrell Froude and the Oxford Movement* (London, Elek, 1974), p. 185.

42 Froude's *Remains*, 1, p. 336.

43 Froude's *Remains*, 1, p. 336.

44 Coleridge, *A Memoir*, p. 255.

45 Froude's *Remains*, 1, p. 322.

46 Froude's *Remains*, 1, p. 322.

47 Chadwick, *The Victorian Church*, 1, p. 175.

48 R. W. Church, *The Oxford Movement: Twelve Years 1833–1845* (London, Macmillan, 1891), p. 42.
49 Froude's *Remains*, 1, Preface, p. xxii.
50 Ker, *Newman*, p. 166.
51 Liddon, *Life of Pusey*, 2, p. 67.
52 Ker, *Newman*, p. 172.
53 Liddon, *Life of Pusey*, 2, p. 66.

4 The End of the Tracts

1 W. J. Conybeare, *Edinburgh Review* 200 (October 1853), p. 302.
2 G. Prevost (ed.), *The Autobiography of Isaac Williams, B.D.* (London, Longmans, Green, 1892), pp. 91–2.
3 Prevost (ed.), *Isaac Williams*, p. 89.
4 Prevost (ed.), *Isaac Williams*, pp. 88–9.
5 Prevost (ed.), *Isaac Williams*, pp. 63–4.
6 R. W. Church, *The Oxford Movement: Twelve Years 1833–1845* (London, Macmillan, 1891), p. 67.
7 Church, *The Oxford Movement*, p. 67.
8 I. Williams, *Tract 80*, 'On Reserve in communicating Religious Knowledge' 1837, but published undated. Quotations from *Tracts for The Times*, 4 (1836–7; new edn, London, 1840), p. 3.
9 Williams, *Tract 80*, p. 5.
10 Williams, *Tract 80*, p. 29.
11 H. Chadwick, 'Newman's significance for the Anglican Church', in D. Brown (ed.), *Newman: A Man for Our Own Time: Centenary Essays* (London, SPCK, 1990), p. 66.
12 J. H. Newman, *Tract 90*, p. 98. References are to the 1841 edn, repr. with a historical introduction by A. W. Evans (London, Constable, 1933).
13 Newman, *Tract 90*, p. 99.
14 Newman, *Tract 90*, p. 100.
15 Church, *The Oxford Movement*, p. 267.
16 Books of Homilies were issued in the reign of King Edward VI and Queen Elizabeth I to provide authorized teaching to be read in churches where parish clergy were either illiterate or unwilling to preach orthodox sermons. The Homilies are listed in Article 35.
17 The Schoolmen were the theologians who worked in the tradition of the 'Medieval Schools' which defined orthodoxy. The work of St Thomas Aquinas was the crowning achievement of the Schoolmen.
18 Church, *The Oxford Movement*, p. 290.

19 Church, *The Oxford Movement*, p. 296.

20 H. P. Liddon, *The Life of E. B. Pusey, D.D.* (London, Longmans, Green, 1893–7), 2, p. 168.

21 I. Ker, *John Henry Newman: A Biography* (Oxford, Oxford University Press, 1988), p. 221.

22 R. T. Davidson and W. Benham, *Life of Archibald Campbell Tait, Archbishop of Canterbury* (London, Macmillan, 1891), 1, p. 86.

23 Davidson and Benham, *Life of Tait*, 1, p. 76.

24 Davidson and Benham, *Life of Tait*, 1, p. 78.

25 Davidson and Benham, *Life of Tait*, 1, p. 95.

26 Liddon, *Life of Pusey*, 2, p. 168 n.

27 Liddon, *Life of Pusey*, 2, p. 170.

28 Quoted by Church, *The Oxford Movement*, pp. 291–2.

29 Richard William Jelf (1798–1871), Canon of Christ Church, Oxford, Bampton Lecturer 1844. Principal of King's College, London. A friend of Pusey's all his life, although they had considerable theological differences of opinion.

30 J. H. Newman, *A Letter addressed to the Rev. R. W. Jelf, D.D.* (Oxford, Henry Parker, 1841), p. 27.

31 Newman, *Letter to Jelf*, p. 29.

32 Quoted in Liddon, *Life of Pusey*, 2, p. 175.

33 O. Chadwick. *The Victorian Church*, 1 (London, A. & C. Black, 1966), p. 181.

34 Davidson and Benham, *Life of Tait*, 1, p. 93.

35 Liddon, *Life of Pusey*, 2, p. 188.

36 Liddon, *Life of Pusey*, 2, p. 184.

37 Liddon, *Life of Pusey*, 2, p. 185.

38 Liddon, *Life of Pusey*, 2, p. 187.

39 Liddon, *Life of Pusey*, 2, pp. 189–90.

40 Liddon, *Life of Pusey*, 2, p. 191.

41 Liddon, *Life of Pusey*, 2, p. 193.

42 Liddon, *Life of Pusey*, 2, p. 194.

43 Liddon, *Life of Pusey*, 2, p. 197.

44 Liddon, *Life of Pusey*, 2, p. 198.

45 Liddon, *Life of Pusey*, 2, p. 199.

46 Liddon, *Life of Pusey*, 2, p. 200.

47 Liddon, *Life of Pusey*, 2, p. 201.

48 J. H. Newman, *A Letter to the Right Reverend Father in God, Richard, Lord Bishop of Oxford* (Oxford, J. H. Parker, 1841), p. 3.

49 Newman, *Letter to the Bishop of Oxford*, pp. 41–2.

50 Newman, *Letter to the Bishop of Oxford*, p. 46.

51 Newman, *Letter to the Bishop of Oxford*, p. 46.
52 Liddon, *Life of Pusey*, 2, p. 236.
53 Liddon, *Life of Pusey*, 2, p. 238.
54 Liddon, *Life of Pusey*, 2, p. 237.
55 Liddon, *Life of Pusey*, 2, p. 240.

5 Contending with Setbacks

1 The *Library of Anglo-Catholic Theology* has not received the attention it deserves from historians of the Oxford Movement. It seems to have been Keble's idea, and he served on the committee which promoted it, but seems to have had a somewhat ambivalent attitude to the series.

2 A quite unexpected parallel to this activity was the work of some opponents of the Tractarians. They decided to make other texts available and in order to do so formed the Parker Society in 1840. This was a Protestant answer to the intellectual work of the Tractarians and produced 'the works of the Fathers and early writers of the Reformed Church'. It was named after the first Archbishop of Canterbury of the reign of Queen Elizabeth I, Matthew Parker, and his work was included in its publications along with that of Archbishop Cranmer and a number of others. As a result, some of the selectiveness of the Tractarians was countered and scholarship benefited across two areas of the theological spectrum.

3 R. W. Church, *The Oxford Movement: Twelve Years 1833–1845* (London, Macmillan, 1891), p. 317.

4 G. Battiscombe, *Shaftesbury: A Biography of the Seventh Earl, 1801–1885* (London, Constable, 1974), p. 140.

5 H. P. Liddon, *The Life of E. B. Pusey, D.D.* (London, Longmans, Green, 1893–7), 2, p. 250.

6 J. H. Newman, *Apologia pro vita sua* (London, Penguin, 1994), p. 140.

7 Quoted in Liddon, *Life of Pusey*, 2, p. 309.

8 Liddon, *Life of Pusey*, 2, p. 312.

9 Liddon, *Life of Pusey*, 2, p. 317.

10 Liddon, *Life of Pusey*, 2, p. 333.

11 Liddon, *Life of Pusey*, 2, p. 346.

12 Liddon, *Life of Pusey*, 2, p. 363.

13 S. Prickett, 'Church and University in the Life of John Keble', in G. Rowell (ed.), *The English Religious Tradition and the Genius of Anglicanism* (Wantage, Ikon, 1992), p. 198.

14 G. Prevost (ed.), *The Autobiography of Isaac Williams, B.D.* (London, Longmans, Green, 1892), p. 137ff.

15 Prevost (ed.), *Isaac Williams*, p. 138.

16 Liddon, *Life of Pusey*, 2, p. 262.

17 Liddon, *Life of Pusey*, 2, p. 231.

18 W. G. Ward, *The Ideal of a Christian Church Considered in Comparison with Existing Practice* (London, J. Toovey, 1844), p. 567.

19 I. Ker, *John Henry Newman: A Biography* (Oxford, Oxford University Press, 1988), p. 296.

20 Church, *The Oxford Movement*, p. 388.

21 Ker, *Newman*, p. 194.

22 Newman, *Apologia*, p. 161.

23 Liddon, *Life of Pusey*, 2, pp. 290–1: the later reference is to pp. 370–1.

24 Liddon, *Life of Pusey*, 2, p. 371.

25 Liddon, *Life of Pusey*, 2, p. 461.

6 'The leaders stood firm'

1 R. W. Church, *The Oxford Movement: Twelve Years 1833–1845* (London, Macmillan, 1891), p. 396.

2 H. P. Liddon, *The Life of E. B. Pusey, D.D.* (London, Longmans, Green, 1893–7), 2, pp. 456, 457.

3 G. Herring, *What was the Oxford Movement?* (London, Continuum, 2002), pp. 69–71.

4 W. Lock, *John Keble: A Biography* (London, Methuen, 1893), pp. 142–3.

5 Lock, *Keble*, p. 144.

6 Quoted in O. Chadwick, *The Spirit of the Oxford Movement: Tractarian Essays* (Cambridge, Cambridge University Press, 1990), p. 62.

7 P. G. Cobb, 'Leader of the Anglo-Catholics', in P. Butler (ed.), *Pusey Rediscovered* (London, SPCK, 1983), pp. 349–65, p. 349.

8 W. Palmer, *A Narrative of Events connected with the publication of the Tracts for the Times* (enlarged edn, London, Rivingtons, 1883), p. 240.

9 Liddon, *Life of Pusey*, 2, p. 462. The full text of the letter can be found on pp. 460–3.

10 Liddon, *Life of Pusey*, 2, p. 462.

11 Herring, *What was the Oxford Movement?*, p. 69.

12 F. Knight, 'The Influence of the Oxford Movement in the Parishes, c. 1833–1860, a Reassessment', in P. Vaiss (ed.), *From Oxford to the People: Reconsidering Newman and the Oxford Movement* (Leominster, Gracewing, 1996), pp. 127–40, see p. 128.

13 A. P. Perceval, *A Collection of Papers connected with the Theological Movement of 1833* (London, Rivington, etc., 1842), p. 20.

14 W. R. W. Stephens, *The Life and Letters of Walter Farquhar Hook* (new edn, London, Bentley, 1880) p. 399.

15 Stephens, *Hook*, p. 593.

16 A. M. Allchin, *The Silent Rebellion: Anglican Religious Communities, 1845–1900* (London, SCM Press, 1958), p. 37, quoting Liddon's biography of Hamilton, p. 13.

17 Allchin, *The Silent Rebellion*, pp. 37ff.

18 Liddon, *Life of Pusey*, 3, p. 247.

19 Liddon, *Life of Pusey*, 3, p. 343.

20 Liddon, *Life of Pusey*, 3, p. 430.

21 Herring, *What was the Oxford Movement?*, p. 71.

22 G. Battiscombe, *John Keble: A Study in Limitations* (London, Constable, 1963), p. 302.

23 Liddon, *Life of Pusey*, 3, p. 239.

24 O. Chadwick, *The Victorian Church*, 1 (London, A. & C. Black, 1966), p 292.

25 Liddon, *Life of Pusey*, 3, p. 291.

26 Liddon, *Life of Pusey*, 3, p. 140.

27 Quoted in Chadwick, *The Victorian Church*, 1, p. 301.

7 'Ritualism and Ritual'

1 W. E. Gladstone, 'Ritual and Ritualism', the title of an article in *Contemporary Review* 24 (1874), pp. 663–81.

2 H. P. Liddon, The *Life of E. B. Pusey, D.D.* (London, Longmans, Green, 1893–7), 3, p. 369.

3 N. Yates, *Anglican Ritualism in Victorian Britain: 1830–1910* (Oxford, Clarendon Press, 1999), p. 44.

4 Gladstone, 'Ritual and Ritualism', p. 677.

5 Gladstone, 'Ritual and Ritualism', p. 681.

6 R. W. Church, *The Oxford Movement: Twelve Years 1833–1845* (London, Macmillan, 1891), p. 371.

7 S. L. Ollard, *A Short History of the Oxford Movement* (London, Mowbray, 1915; repr. 1983), p. 159.

8 Quoted by J. Bentley, *Ritualism and Politics in Victorian Britain: The Attempt to Legislate for Belief* (Oxford, Oxford University Press, 1978), p. 26.

9 Mary Church, *The Life and Letters of Dean Church* (London, Macmillan, 1895), p. 172.

10 Yates, *Anglican Ritualism*, p. 218.
11 G. Herring, *What was the Oxford Movement?* (London, Continuum, 2002), p. 72.
12 G. Battiscombe, *John Keble: A Study in Limitations* (London, Constable, 1963), p. 350.
13 Bentley, *Ritualism and Politics*, p. 44.
14 J. S. Reed, *Glorious Battle: The Cultural Politics of Victorian Anglo-Catholicism* (Nashville, TN, Vanderbilt University Press, 1996; repr. London, Tufton Books, 1998), p. 238.
15 Reed, *Glorious Battle*, p. 239.
16 P. B. Nockles, *The Oxford Movement in Context: Anglican High Churchmanship 1760–1857* (Cambridge, Cambridge University Press, 1994), p. 253.
17 Quoted by O. Chadwick, *The Mind of the Oxford Movement* (London, A. & C. Black, 1960), p. 200.
18 D. A. R. Forrester, *Young Dr Pusey: A Study in Development* (London, Mowbray, 1989), pp. 200–1.
19 Quoted by Bentley, *Ritualism and Politics*, p. 31.
20 Quoted by Bentley, *Ritualism and Politics*, p. 31.
21 A. Clifton Kelway, *George Rundle Prynne: A Chapter in the Early History of the Catholic Revival* (London, Longmans, 1905), p. 74.
22 Gladstone, 'Ritualism and Ritual', p. 679.

8 Last Words

1 J. A. Froude, *Short Studies on Great Subjects* (London, Longmans, Green, 1894), 4, p. 267.
2 G. Battiscombe, *John Keble: A Study in Limitations* (London, Constable, 1963), p. 353.
3 Mary Church, *The Life and Letters of Dean Church* (London, Macmillan, 1895), p. 172.
4 Quoted in H. P. Liddon, *The Life of E. B. Pusey, D.D.* (London, Longmans, Green, 1893–7), 4, p. 389.
5 Liddon, *Life of Pusey*, 4, p. 387.
6 C. Gore (ed.), *Lux Mundi: A Series of Studies in the Religion of the Incarnation* (London, John Murray, 1889), preface, p. vii.
7 J. A. Froude, *Short Studies on Great Subjects* (London, Longmans, Green, 1894), 4, p. 310.
8 S. L. Ollard, *A Short History of the Oxford Movement* (London, Mowbray 1915; repr. 1983), pp. 140, 151.

Select Bibliography

An immense amount has been written about the Oxford Movement, and no bibliography can be more than a selection which may assist further reading. This list includes some nineteenth-century publications with more accessible and recently published material. There are some additional items mentioned in the footnotes.

Biographies of John Keble

Battiscombe, G., *John Keble: A Study in Limitations* (London, Constable, 1963)

Coleridge, J. T., *A Memoir of the Reverend John Keble, M.A.* (Oxford, Parker, 1870)

Wood, E. F. L., *Leaders of the Church 1800–1900: John Keble* (London, Mowbray, 1909)

Biographies of Edward Bouverie Pusey

Butler, P. (ed.), *Pusey Rediscovered* (London, SPCK, 1983)

Liddon, H. P., *The Life of E. B. Pusey, D.D.* (London, Longmans, Green, 4 vol., 1893–7)

Biographies of John Henry Newman

Ker, I., *John Henry Newman: A Biography* (Oxford, Oxford University Press, 1988)

Newman, J. H., *Apologia pro vita sua* (1864; repr. London, Penguin, 1994)

Other biographies

Brendon, P., *Hurrell Froude and the Oxford Movement* (London, Elek, 1974)

Prevost, G. (ed.), *The Autobiography of Isaac Williams, B.D.* (London, Longmans, Green, 1892)

Ward, W., *William George Ward and the Oxford Movement* (London, Macmillan, 1889, repr. 1969)

Histories and commentaries

Bentley, J., *Ritualism and Politics in Victorian Britain: The Attempt to Legislate for Belief* (Oxford, Oxford University Press, 1978)

Brilioth, Y., *The Anglican Revival: Studies in the Oxford Movement* (London, Longmans, Green, 1933)

Chadwick, O., *The Mind of the Oxford Movement* (London, A. & C. Black, 1960)

Chadwick, O., *The Spirit of the Oxford Movement: Tractarian Essays* (Cambridge, Cambridge University Press, 1990)

Chadwick, O., *The Victorian Church* (London, A. & C. Black, Part 1, 1966; Part 2, 1970; repr. London, SCM Press, 1987)

Church, R. W., *The Oxford Movement: Twelve Years 1833–1845* (London, Macmillan, 1891)

Fairweather, E. R. (ed.), *The Oxford Movement* (New York, Oxford University Press, 1964)

Hardelin, A., *The Tractarian Understanding of the Eucharist* (Uppsala, Alqvist & Wiksell, 1965)

Herring, G., *What was the Oxford Movement?* (London, Continuum, 2002)

Hogben, B. and Harrison, J. (eds.), *The Oxford Movement: Nineteenth-Century Books and Pamphlets in Canterbury Cathedral Library*, Canterbury Sources, No. 1 (Canterbury, Dean and Chapter of Canterbury, 1999)

Mozley, T., *Reminiscences, Chiefly of Oriel College and the Oxford Movement* (two volumes, London, Longmans, Green, 1882)

Nockles, P. B., *The Oxford Movement in Context: Anglican High Churchmanship 1760–1857* (Cambridge, Cambridge University Press, 1994)

Ollard, S. L., *A Short History of the Oxford Movement* (London, Mowbray, 1915, repr. 1983)

Palmer, W., *A Narrative of Events connected with the publication of the Tracts for the Times* (Oxford, J. H. Parker, 1843; enlarged with an Introduction and Supplement, London, Rivingtons, 1883)

Perceval, A. P., *A Collection of Papers connected with the Theological Movement of 1833* (London, Rivington, etc., 1842)

Reed, J. S., *Glorious Battle: The Cultural Politics of Victorian Anglo-Catholicism* (Nashville, TN, Vanderbilt University Press, 1996; repr. London, Tufton Books, 1998)

Rowell, G., *The Vision Glorious: Themes and Personalities of the Catholic Revival in Anglicanism* (Oxford, Oxford University Press, 1983)

Rowell, G. (ed.), *Tradition Renewed: The Oxford Movement Conference Papers* (London, Darton, Longman & Todd, 1986)

Vaiss, P. (ed.), *From Oxford to the People: Reconsidering Newman and the Oxford Movement* (Leominster, Gracewing, 1996)

Yates, N., *Anglican Ritualism in Victorian Britain: 1830–1910* (Oxford, Clarendon Press, 1999)

Index